Powerful Literacy in the Montessori Classroom

Aligning Reading Research and Practice

Susan Zoll, Natasha Feinberg, and Laura Saylor

Foreword by Daniel Willingham
and Trisha Thompson-Willingham

TEACHERS COLLEGE PRESS

TEACHERS COLLEGE | COLUMBIA UNIVERSITY
NEW YORK AND LONDON

Published by Teachers College Press,® 1234 Amsterdam Avenue, New York, NY 10027

Cover art by Drinevskaya Olga via Shutterstock.

The cards in Table 7.1 are copyright Association Montessori Internationale (AMI) and published via their website montessoridigital.org.

Library of Congress Cataloging-in-Publication Data

Names: Zoll, Susan, author. | Feinberg, Natasha, author. | Saylor, Laura, author.
Title: Powerful literacy in the Montessori classroom : aligning reading research and practice / Susan Zoll, Natasha Feinberg, and Laura Saylor ; foreword by Daniel Willingham and Trisha Thompson-Willingham.
Description: New York, NY : Teachers College Press, 2023. | Includes bibliographical references and index. | Summary: "This book aligns Montessori didactic materials and pedagogy with current research on reading development. Readers will gain a solid overview of the Montessori philosophy and method, specifically those related to reading and language development, enabling them to support their practice in today's educational context (preschool to grade 3)"— Provided by publisher.
Identifiers: LCCN 2022038133 (print) | LCCN 2022038134 (ebook) | ISBN 9780807768389 (paperback) | ISBN 9780807768396 (hardback) | ISBN 9780807781746 (ebook)
Subjects: LCSH: Reading (Preschool) | Reading (Elementary) | Montessori method of education.
Classification: LCC LB1140.5.R4 Z65 2023 (print) | LCC LB1140.5.R4 (ebook) | DDC 372.4—dc23/eng/20220922
LC record available at https://lccn.loc.gov/2022038133
LC ebook record available at https://lccn.loc.gov/2022038134

ISBN 978-0-8077-6838-9 (paper)
ISBN 978-0-8077-6839-6 (hardcover)
ISBN 978-0-8077-8174-6 (ebook)

Printed on acid-free paper

Manufactured in the United States of America

To Barry, Hannah, Sierra, Rachel, and Patricia—you have taught me the value of a life well-lived.

And many thanks to the educators who transform lines on a page to worlds of information and imagination for every learner.
—Susan Zoll

To Dan, Yalith, Mom, and Dad
You are an amazing support team and terrific cheerleaders.
I love you all!
—Natasha Feinberg

To Bud and Toni; Andi and Hank; and Joey
And to my family of colleagues.
Your love, generosity, and grace make my work possible.
—Laura Saylor

Contents

Foreword

Americans are reliably pessimistic about the state of reading in their country, and indeed, it seems there's nothing connected to reading to be proud of. Children and adults read very little in their leisure time. American students of all ages don't read well, as assessed by international comparison tests, or by our own National Assessment of Educational Progress, often called "The Nation's Report Card." Reading achievement for economically disadvantaged children continues to lag far behind that of wealthy children.

This concern is well-placed, as reading is the keystone to the rest of education. As children get older, teachers set higher and higher expectations about how much students can learn on their own via independent reading. The students who struggle to read are left further and further behind.

Although observers of American education have been anxious about reading and have been open to new ideas to improve—sometimes indiscriminately open—they have mostly remained oblivious to two potentially valuable sources of guidance: the Montessori method and the scientific study of reading.

The scientific study of how children learn to read, the best way to teach it, and how the process of reading changes as readers gain expertise has been under way for more than a century. These are challenging scientific questions, but the effort has been enormous, and real progress has been made on many key aspects of each problem. Still, the science of reading is frequently portrayed as uncertain and speculative. Those who don't follow the research closely often think it only addresses decoding.

Montessori education offers an altogether different source of information for educators—a working example that might be emulated. Montessori schools in the United States have used the same method to teach reading since their inception in the early 20th century. Although advocates have always claimed that the method was highly successful and anecdotal evidence was plentiful, it was not until the early part of this century that systematic data were collected, showing that Montessori schools compared favorably with traditional schooling.

One of us is a scientist who has written two books about reading, and the other is a Montessori teacher and reading specialist who has taught scores of children to read. How often we have thought, "someone really ought to write a book that shows how these perspectives go together!"

And now Susan Zoll, Natasha Feinberg, and Laura Saylor have done so. With *Powerful Literacy in the Montessori Classroom: Aligning Reading Research and Practice*, readers can learn from both of these exceptional sources of information about literacy. The authors take the reader on a journey through *all* aspects of reading—a depth most books cannot match—showing how each component is handled in a Montessori classroom, and how that pedagogy aligns with scientific findings.

Everyone will find something of value to them here.

Not only will Montessori teachers come to understand the science of reading, they will also find a useful review of their practice, coupled with a new depth of understanding. They know that what they do works, and now they'll know why; the matrix[1] (which coordinates the scientific principles with Montessori materials) is especially helpful to reach this understanding. This book will also acquaint Montessorians with the literacy terms and frames of reference used outside Montessori schools, which is important in communicating with reading specialists and parents. Come to that, this book would be ideal for Montessori parents who are curious to understand how their child will learn to read.

Like Montessorians, teachers in traditional schools will appreciate the thorough yet approachable review of the science of reading. They will also find great value in the description of the Montessori method of teaching reading. At the very least, it will prove useful in understanding what a child who moves to a traditional school from a Montessori school has been exposed to; still better, we think it's a treasure trove of practical ideas for teachers and reading specialists at traditional schools.

Policymakers, too, will profit from reading this volume—if they despair at the poor reading performance of American children and wish for a method of teaching reading that is rooted in science and practicable *today*, they need look no further.

Zoll, Feinberg, and Saylor have done a signal job of explaining two complex sets of ideas with clarity and flair. Read, enjoy, and profit!

Daniel T. Willingham and Trisha Thompson-Willingham

---

1. To access the *Montessori Materials and Science of Reading Matrix*, please see the QR code and link listed in the Conclusion (Chapter 11) of this book.

Welcome

In this book, we welcome you to share our exploration of two influential methods of literacy instruction that mold the youth we serve: Montessori and the Science of Reading. As authors, we bring to this book our unique experiences as educators and researchers. Two of us are trained in Montessori education and one as a traditional elementary school teacher. We are all immersed in current reading research and focused on celebrating and strengthening the amazing instruction that occurs daily in classrooms around the world. Throughout our writing endeavors, we have challenged one another to discuss and examine the intersection of these two areas of pedagogy, Montessori and the Science of Reading, both of which offer significant contributions to best practices in the classroom. In this process, we have discovered the many overlapping instructional approaches as well as the additional contributions that Montessori and current reading research offer to each other. It is our hope that you, too, will be inspired to see the many ways in which Montessori instruction reflects what has been shown by research to be effective literacy instruction and that you will be open to the new learnings that have emerged in the field of education.

Preface

Powerful Literacy in the Montessori Classroom: Aligning Reading Research and Practice offers the reader a view of Montessori education, a learner-centered paradigm developed over a century ago by Dr. Maria Montessori. It also offers the reader an overview of reading research, currently identified as the Science of Reading, providing explicit connections with the materials and instructional approaches used in Montessori classrooms today.

You may be reading this book because you're a student in a Montessori teacher education program studying the Language component of the Montessori curriculum. This book offers rich examples of Montessori instruction and teaching practices that align with evidence-based instruction to ensure that your students become competent readers.

Or perhaps you're a seasoned classroom educator teaching in a publicly funded Montessori charter school or a faculty member responsible for preparing future Montessori educators. For you, this book provides a connection to reading research currently influencing education policy in many states across the country and, ultimately, your classroom. Table I provides an overview of state legislation that has recently passed or is currently under consideration related to reading instruction: legislation that will influence higher education's preparation of preservice teachers to include coursework that aligns with the Science of Reading, professional development requirements for inservice educators, knowledge of reading instruction measured by proficiency exams for all educators, and mandated ELA curriculum identified by districts and state departments of education. Each state has determined its own approach to improving students' reading proficiency, so it is important for educators to be aware of local requirements.

We believe the comparative analysis offered in this book builds on empirical studies of Montessori education (Culclasure, 2018; Lillard et al., 2017) and provides further evidence through rich descriptions of the Montessori curriculum, specifically those materials that support students' language and reading development. We hope you will see the familiar in a new way as we translate Language materials and approaches used in Montessori classrooms with evidence-based instructional practices implemented in more conventional learning environments.

Table I. Science of Reading state legislation, adapted from Pondiscio (2021) and Dyslexia (2022)

States that have passed Science of Reading legislation				
States that require or encourage teacher prep programs to teach the science of reading/ dyslexia	States that require teachers to take a reading proficiency exam based on the science of reading	States that require teachers to use Science of Reading–based instruction or require districts to provide Science of Reading–based curriculum	States that require districts to provide, or teachers to attend, Science of Reading professional development	States with legislation currently under review related to Science of Reading and/ or dyslexia instruction that includes reading research (as of 2022)
California	Alabama	Alabama	Arizona	Alaska
Kentucky	Arkansas	Arizona	Colorado	California
Missouri	Kentucky	Colorado	Rhode Island	Connecticut
N. Carolina	N. Carolina	Florida	Texas	Idaho
Oklahoma	Rhode Island	Mississippi		Illinois
W. Virginia	Texas	Texas		Iowa
				Kansas
				Louisiana
				Michigan
				Minnesota
				New Jersey
				New York
				Ohio
				Pennsylvania
				S. Carolina
				Tennessee
				Wyoming

In Chapter 1, the reader is introduced to Montessori education and its multi-age classrooms that support students' learning in math, language, everyday living skills, science, sensory development, fine arts, and cultural studies. Although Montessori education offers learning environments for infants and toddlers through high school, in this book we have focused on language and literacy experiences in early childhood (3–6 years old) and early elementary (6–9 years old) classrooms. The purpose of the book is to share Montessori didactic materials and pedagogy that specifically support language and literacy development. We then align those practices to reading research, most recently referred to as the Science of Reading (Reading League, 2021).

Our intent is not to compare Montessori education with other contemporary approaches to teaching and learning, but to highlight one pedagogy that has been sorely absent from the literature. Since many Montessori texts speak directly to those working in the field, the intent of this book is to create a shared lexicon bridging Montessori terminology with a larger body of education research. This is particularly important for teachers and administrators working in public Montessori schools who balance meeting state education requirements while maintaining fidelity to Montessori pedagogical principles. Our hope is to make Montessori education visible within the larger field of education—and perhaps more widely accepted—by explicitly aligning the materials and instructional approaches in Montessori classrooms with the Science of Reading.

READING RESEARCH

What does it mean to be a good reader? How can educators best support their students' developing literacy skills? A great deal of research over the past 40 years has identified evidence-based instruction that has the greatest impact on students' ability to read fluently and with comprehension. To ground the reader, Chapter 2 provides a brief historical review of three commissioned reports that conducted meta-analyses of hundreds of research studies highlighting key areas of reading development. In 1998, Harvard University scholar Catherine Snow and her colleagues published (1) *Preventing Reading Difficulties in Young Children*, followed by reports from the (2) National Reading Panel (National Institute of Child Health and Human Development [NICHD], 2001) and the (3) National Early Literacy Panel (2008) that offered empirical evidence highlighting literacy skills that served as strong predictors of successful reading (Vukelich & Christie, 2009, p. 8).

Hollis Scarborough's Reading Rope. The framework for the book is based on an image developed by Yale University scholar Hollis Scarborough (2001) informed by the results of her meta-analysis of reading research. The image (see Figure I) lists key skills noted as strands of the Reading Rope. These strands are divided into lower strands for Word Recognition and upper strands for Language Comprehension skills. Classroom instruction must include a systematic scope and sequence of lessons that address each of the reading strands. And instruction must include adequate time for repetition so that students can strengthen these language comprehension and word recognition

Figure I. Hollis Scarborough's Reading Rope, 2001

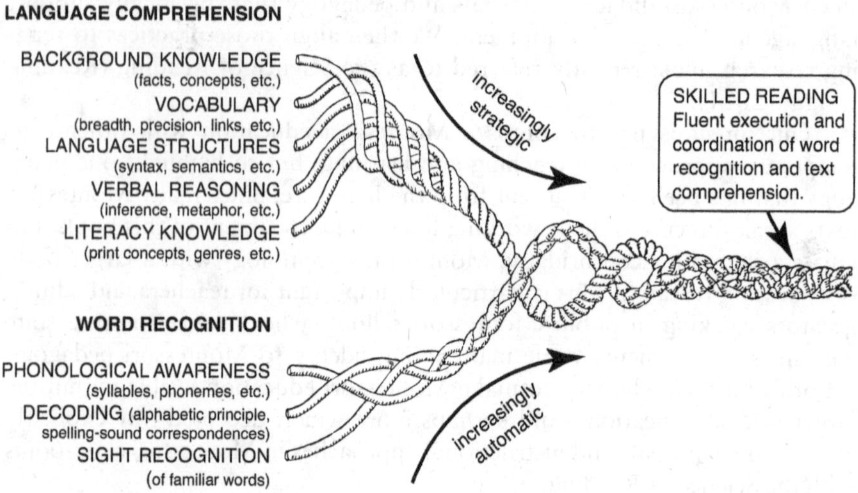

LANGUAGE COMPREHENSION

BACKGROUND KNOWLEDGE
(facts, concepts, etc.)
VOCABULARY
(breadth, precision, links, etc.)
LANGUAGE STRUCTURES
(syntax, semantics, etc.)
VERBAL REASONING
(inference, metaphor, etc.)
LITERACY KNOWLEDGE
(print concepts, genres, etc.)

increasingly strategic

SKILLED READING
Fluent execution and coordination of word recognition and text comprehension.

WORD RECOGNITION

PHONOLOGICAL AWARENESS
(syllables, phonemes, etc.)
DECODING (alphabetic principle, spelling-sound correspondences)
SIGHT RECOGNITION
(of familiar words)

increasingly automatic

Used with permission from Guilford Press.

skills. Ultimately, all students read with fluency and comprehension to ensure their academic success.

Scarborough's Reading Rope offers a comprehensive framework that is informed by research consensus and serves as a guide to exploring the alignment between Montessori education and the Science of Reading. The authors are fully aware of the "reading wars" and the politicization of reading practices. The focus is not on any side or party, but rather on showcasing reading and literacy practices that are evidenced by the body of research that have been shown to work in *all* communities regardless of their socioeconomic or racial demographics. To be a competent reader, children must have access to education designed to develop their talents and personalities, because a student's reading competency is foundational to being prepared to live a fully engaged life in society (United Nations, Convention on the Rights of the Child, Article 29, 1989).

The authors' intent is to serve as a resource that will:

- Open the door to respectful dialogue informed by the body of scientific literature;
- Highlight alignment between Montessori education and the Science of Reading; and
- Provide examples of additional research-based instructional practices for readers to consider within their unique context.

Each chapter begins with an overview of the literacy strand, noting important studies and terminology. This is followed by descriptions of Montessori materials that specifically align to the reading strand and its relevant research. And recognizing the diversity and range of skills found in any classroom, each chapter concludes with additional instructional strategies to meet the needs of all learners. The activities offer educators research-based activities that can supplement Montessori lessons, especially for those students who need additional support in becoming competent readers.

Just as Scarborough's Reading Rope is labeled in two main categories, Part I of this book focuses on activities supporting the Word Recognition portion of Scarborough's Reading Rope, including phonological awareness (Chapter 3), decoding (Chapter 4), and sight recognition (Chapter 5). These three skills allow an individual to unlock a word by turning the symbols on the page into a meaningful word unit. According to Scarborough (2001), when some children struggle to learn to read it is often a lack of mastery of skills identified in these Word Recognition strands.

In Part II, we highlight Montessori materials that support Language Comprehension, including lessons focused on background knowledge (Chapter 6), vocabulary (Chapter 7), language structures (Chapter 8), verbal reasoning (Chapter 9), and literacy knowledge (Chapter 10) strands of the Reading Rope.

Ultimately, it is our hope this book extends your understanding of reading instruction and helps you recognize in a new way the richness of Maria Montessori's integrated curriculum. Language and literacy learning is found in all areas of the classroom. May you be empowered by reading research that aligns to Montessori practice.

> Any teacher, any student, any reader, any writer, sufficiently attentive and motivated, must be able to engage freely with subjects of their choice. That is not only the essence of learning; it's the essence of being human.
> —Henry Louis Gates, Jr. 2021, *New York Times*

Acknowledgments

The authors wish to thank our editor, Emily Spangler, for her encouragement, concise feedback, and incredibly responsive guidance in completing this book. We are grateful to Teachers College Press for their dedication to all educators and their willingness to add a book focused on Montessori education to their expansive library.

We are also grateful for the research conducted by Dr. Hollis Scarborough, and her publisher, Guilford Press, for granting permission to use Scarborough's Reading Rope (2001), which informed the framework for this book.

We are extremely grateful to Chris Willemsen, Heutink International, and Neinhuis Montessori for their generous contribution of time, valuable insight, and use of many Montessori material images included in this book.

We also wish to thank the Association Montessori Internationale (AMI), specifically Lynne Lawrence, Executive Director, and Elske Voermans, Educateurs sans Frontières Coordinator, for the use of their classification cards generously made available to all families and educators in response to the challenges created by COVID-19.

We would additionally like to express our deep appreciation to Daniel Willingham and Trisha Thompson-Willingham for their Foreword to this book. When they accepted our request to write the Foreword, we were so excited. When we read what the two of them wrote, we were touched, humbled, and overjoyed to have our work viewed so positively by people we admire.

And we wish to acknowledge the leadership of the American Montessori Society (AMS), Munir Shivji, Executive Director; Montessori Public Policy Initiative (MPPI) Wendy Shenk-Evans, Executive Director, Denise Monnier, Director of State Advocacy, and Vyju Kadambi, State Advocacy Associate; the National Center for Montessori in the Public Sector (NCMPS), specifically Katie Brown, Director of Research and Professional Learning, and David Ayer, Director of Communications, for their insights, collegiality, and dedication to advocacy on behalf of the Montessori administrators and educators who are working to meet state Science of Reading requirements.

Many thanks to our mentors in the field: Susan Egan, Joyce Butler, Ann Laughlin, Amy Murdoch, and to the many children in our classrooms who often served as our best teachers in becoming effective educators. And finally, on behalf of Montessori educators and administrators—and the children and families they serve across the globe—we are deeply appreciative for the work of Dr. Maria Montessori and her vision in transforming education.

Lastly, Natasha and Laura would like to acknowledge this book's first author, their trusted colleague and dear friend, Susan Zoll. Susan's vision, commitment, and leadership made this book both a possibility and a reality!

CHAPTER 1

Montessori Education

There are many books that describe the early years of Dr. Maria Montessori's career. For the purpose of this book, the authors provide a brief overview of the Montessori pedagogy and its application in classrooms globally over the last hundred years, with a particular focus on those attributes of Dr. Montessori's work that most align to current evidence-based practices in education.

DR. MARIA MONTESSORI

Women in the early 1900s had few career options, but with the support of her family, a determined Maria Montessori was one of the first women in Italy to earn her medical degree. The journey was not easy, as she was often required to complete assignments, such as conducting autopsies on human cadavers, at a different time and location from her male colleagues. Even the medical opportunities available for her to conduct her required research were significantly narrowed. Ultimately, Dr. Montessori focused on working with young children who displayed intellectual disabilities. To better understand their learning and development, she applied a scientific approach to conducting child observations. Outcomes of these observations informed a new child-centered pedagogy of education that was applied to typically developing children who lived in marginalized communities in Rome. At the request of a local community developer who designed a new apartment building in Rome, Dr. Montessori opened the doors of the first Casa dei Bambini, or Children's House, in 1907. While parents worked, their 3- to 7-year-old children who lived in the tenement would spend their day in Dr. Montessori's classroom in the basement of the building. It was a learning environment for the children, as well as a type of laboratory for Dr. Montessori and the other educators who served them.

Interest in this new approach to teaching and learning grew throughout Europe. By 1911, *McClure's* magazine helped build a strong following for Montessori education in the United States. This popular publication dedicated several issues to the new pedagogy and the woman who created it. Public interest in Dr. Montessori's work was so high that Maria hosted the

Figure 1.1. Assumed Participants of Dr. Montessori's First International Training, Rome, Italy, 1913

Photo courtesy of Rhode Island Normal School Memorabilia, College Archives, Special Collections, James P. Adams Library, Rhode Island College.

first international training in Rome from January through May of 1913. More than 80 participants attended from around the world (Figure 1.1). One participant, Clara Craig from the Rhode Island Normal School, a teacher preparation program, was sent to the training for the sole purpose of determining if the Montessori method was an effective approach for teaching reading to newly immigrated children who spoke a language other than English in their home (Zoll, 2017). Archived reports submitted to the Rhode Island Department of Education, 3 years after Craig created an experimental Montessori program, noted impressive student outcomes:

> Several children, having been trained in this school and having attained the age of six years, are now candidates for the primary department. These children, even now, excel, by far, the prescribed attainment of children who have progressed beyond regular first grade work. They are attracting the curious interest of expert educators. (Rhode Island Board of Education, 1917, p. a23)

In December 1913, Dr. Montessori traveled to the United States to meet with some of her newly trained Montessori teachers. Her itinerary was filled with multiple meetings each day. She spoke at two sold-out engagements at Carnegie Hall and shared movie reels showcasing children's learning in her classrooms.

The Montessori materials and approach to teaching drew from the work of counterparts in developmental psychology and education (Séguin, Itard, and Froebel). The pedagogy reflected learning from Dr. Montessori's ongoing detailed observations of children, how children responded to their classroom environment, and their innate desire to be engaged in authentic learning activities, as well as the educator's role in preparing such an environment.

The Montessori method differed from conventional education, as it personalized instruction and offered students a structured and systematic progression of content across all learning domains. Rather than information being transferred from the adult to students, Dr. Montessori envisioned a reciprocal relationship between the educator, the student, and the learning environment. In the next section the authors consider the growth of Montessori education, and then explore the design of Montessori materials and their use in the classroom.

GROWTH OF MONTESSORI EDUCATION

One of the most difficult tasks we face as human beings is communicating meaning across our individual differences, a task confounded immeasurably when we attempt to communicate across social lines, racial lines, cultural lines, or lines of unequal power. Yet, all U.S. demographic data points to a society becoming increasingly diverse, and that diversity is nowhere more evident than in our schools.
                                                                  —Lisa Delpit, 2006, p. 66

Today, interest in the Montessori approach has grown from private school settings to growing numbers of public school classrooms across the country. According to the National Census (National Center for Montessori in the Public Sector, 2021), there are 20,000 Montessori schools globally, including 3,000 in the United States, of which 560 are publicly funded schools that have adopted the pedagogy. Over the last decade, private funding has also fueled the expansion of Montessori education, increasing access through neighborhood microschools situated in underresourced communities (Walton Family Foundation, 2018).

Mira Debs (2019), a Yale University researcher, identified Montessori schools as the "dominant alternative pedagogy in the public sector" (p. 10), significantly outnumbering Waldorf and Reggio Emilia–inspired schools. Debs noted that progressive pedagogies like Montessori, which are focused on creating racially and socioeconomically diverse and inclusive schools, recognize the innate potential of each child and focus on individualized learning, both supporting and validating children from a wide range of backgrounds (p. 9).

In her demographic analysis of 300 schoolwide public Montessori programs, nearly half of the schools were situated in urban settings, with student enrollment that was highly diverse both racially and socioeconomically.

The Montessori curriculum embraces multiculturalism, and research points to its "positive impact on student achievement if implemented comprehensively . . . and includes consideration for the languages, customs, values, and experiences of all students—not just the dominant culture" (Canzoneri-Golden & King, 2020, p. 27). This appreciation of culture can be found in Montessori materials such as world maps and flags (Figure 1.2) and three-part

Figure 1.2. The Continent Globe and Map, and Continent Animal Box

Image courtesy of Nienhuis Montessori.

picture or nomenclature cards, as well as objects representing lived and studied cultures. History, geography, and culture in a Montessori classroom are not separate curricula but, rather, embedded components of learning.

MONTESSORI MATERIALS AND THE PREPARED ENVIRONMENT

The materials, learning environment, and personalized instructional approach are key components of the Montessori pedagogy. In fact, wherever one finds themselves in the world, a Montessori classroom can be easily identified by the many shared environmental features, including the instructional materials designed by Dr. Montessori to enhance students' learning and development in math, practical life, sensorial, cultural, and language domains. Rather than textbooks and worksheets, the classroom serves as a living curriculum. Montessori materials are organized on shelves in a left-to-right, top-to-bottom progression. Students are invited to lessons, moving systematically from concrete introductory activities to more abstract advanced materials.

Dr. Montessori designed each material to *isolate the difficulty* of its learning objective. While students self-select materials, behind the selection there is an artful influence from the teacher supporting their choice. After initial lessons, students return to practice newly acquired skills and work independently of the teacher (who is always observing). The materials ingeniously contain an internal *control of error,* allowing the student to self-assess if an activity has been completed with accuracy. For example, Knobbed Cylinders (Figure 1.3) offer a didactic experience of ordering, pairing, sorting, and grading. The material isolates the height and width of each cylinder, and its control of error is that there is only one correct space in which each knobbed cylinder can be placed.

The carefully prepared learning environment is designed with intentionally situated learning areas for individual and small-group work. Though

Figure 1.3. Knobbed Cylinders

Image courtesy of Nienhuis Montessori.

classroom walls may showcase select art images, they are usually free of charts and other conventional learning tools. There is a general hum of children's activity and work in the classroom, yet the tone remains subdued, as students are engaged in meaningful activities, and teachers move about the room to offer differentiated instruction based on individual student needs.

The physical and aesthetic characteristics of learning environments influence student engagement. Outcomes of a study conducted by Peter Barrett and his colleagues (2013) identified five distinct classroom design elements that were found to improve student learning: color, choice, complexity, flexibility, and light (p. 682). Next, the authors describe each of the study's design elements and align them with characteristics of Montessori learning environments.

- **Color.** In the study, the selection of neutral palettes on classroom walls, floors, furniture, and displays contributed to older students' ability to concentrate. In a Montessori classroom, the learning environment is usually more subdued, with neutral wall and furniture colors. Instead, it is the color of the Montessori materials that draw students' attention, such as the Pink Tower (Figure 1.4) or the blue Geometric Solids (Figure 1.5). As with most of her pedagogical decisions, Dr. Montessori selected colors for her materials based on observations of which colors children selected more frequently when engaging with her materials (Brunold-Conesa, 2021).
- **Choice.** The degree to which students felt a sense of ownership of their classroom also influenced students' learning. In a Montessori classroom, students share a responsibility for the care and upkeep of the environment. The classroom does not belong to the teacher, and in fact there is often no "teacher's desk" to be found in the room. Rather, the entire classroom is designed for the students' use, which supports this feeling of ownership.
- **Complexity.** The degree to which the classroom environment offers complexity is of importance. The interior design of the room can attract the students' attention, but the design must also be balanced with a sense of order. The well-designed Montessori classroom is organized with every material serving a purpose. Clutter or visual noise is avoided. Since the classroom contains materials for students within a 3-year age span (e.g., 3–6, 6–9), the shelves have a wide progression of curriculum with which to engage.

    For example, in a primary (3–6) classroom, activities include introductory letter and number lessons with the Sandpaper Letters (Figure 1.6) and Number Rods (Figure 1.7). Both introductory lessons offer tactile learning experiences for the youngest preschool students. Sandpaper Letters help students learn letter shapes and their respective letter sounds as they lightly trace with their finger each letter outlined

Figure 1.4. Pink Tower

Image courtesy of Nienhuis Montessori.

Figure 1.5. Geometric Solids

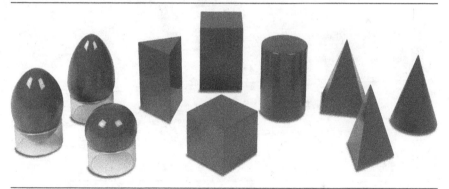

Image courtesy of Nienhuis Montessori.

with fine-grained sandpaper (additional information can be found in Chapter 4). The Number Rods include 10 alternately painted red and blue wooden rods. Each rod differs in length by 10 cm from the preceding rod. The material supports mathematical understanding of numbers 1–10, as well as math language "greater than," "less than," and "equal to" when comparing the rods.

Figure 1.6. Sandpaper Letters

Image courtesy of Nienhuis Montessori.

Figure 1.7. Number Rods

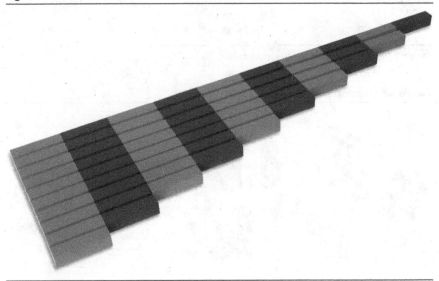

Image courtesy of Nienhuis Montessori.

As students progress to more advanced activities, 6-year-old students work with Phonogram Cards (Figure 1.8) to reinforce reading of non-phonetic word patterns (additional information can be found in Chapter 5). More abstract math materials such as the Stamp Game (Figure 1.9) are available for students to individually practice addition, subtraction, multiplication, and division computational skills.

Figure 1.8. Phonogram Cards

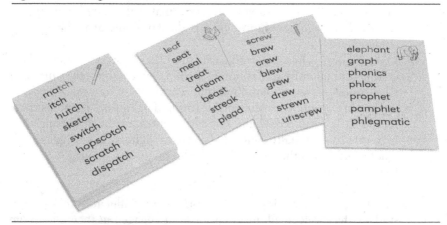

Image courtesy of Nienhuis Montessori.

Figure 1.9. The Stamp Game

Image courtesy of Nienhuis Montessori.

This is just a small sample of the range of materials in a Montessori classroom that creates structured complexity within a learning environment. Students begin where they are in their learning and progress at their own pace through scaffolded lessons across all learning domains.

- **Flexibility.** Flexibility allows for diverse learning areas, classroom environments where students have space to interact and yet not feel crowded. In a Montessori classroom, students have opportunities to move freely about the room and to work individually or in small groups at nearby tables or on floor mats. The classroom is divided into sections based on subject area, and materials related to math, science, language, geography, etc. are displayed and available for students' use.

- **Light.** Though often out of the control of the classroom teacher, the quality and quantity of natural daylight a classroom receives matters. Classrooms with large windows that access lots of natural daylight can positively influence students' learning. For those classrooms that receive little natural daylight, this can be mediated by dispersing high-quality, manually controlled electrical lighting in key areas where students gather or work in the learning environment. (Barrett et al., 2013, p. 688)

Collectively, these complex, multisensory factors influence the degree to which students feel welcomed, inspired, or even engaged in their classroom environment.

THE MONTESSORI EDUCATOR'S APPROACH TO INSTRUCTION

In all classroom settings (ages 0–3, 3–6, 6–9, 9–12, as well as junior and senior high school), lessons in a Montessori classroom are presented in a structured progression. Math, language, science, and geography lessons provide opportunities to build rich background knowledge (Chapter 7) and vocabulary (Chapter 8) that will later support reading and writing development. Dr. Montessori believed a teacher "must be filled with wonder . . . It is not enough for you to love the child. You must first love and understand the universe. You must prepare yourself and truly work at it" (Standing, 1957/1998, p. 309). In teacher preparation, Montessori educators are provided with pedagogical and content information, but the true work was in reflecting on one's character, identity, and spirit (Montessori, 1949/1967, p. 95). "In other words, the path to becoming filled with grandeur or wonder, and being able to transmit this to the child, involves intimate self-knowledge; in a non-religious sense, it requires a spiritual transformation" (Rathunde, 2015, p. 19).

In the early 1900s, students' desks and chairs were often nailed to the floor, causing Dr. Montessori to remark "in such a school the children, like butterflies mounted on pins, are fastened each to his place, the desk, spreading the useless wings of barren and meaningless knowledge which they have acquired" (Montessori, 1948/1967, p. 11). Instruction was static and student engagement limited.

From the earliest Montessori classrooms in San Lorenzo, Italy, students had *freedom* to self-select work and to remain with their lessons for extended periods of time. Teachers present materials that engage students' senses and guide their work selection while promoting movement throughout the class-room. Hallmarks of Montessori instruction include greater attention to model-ing a lesson with limited verbal delivery. Instruction is systematic, explicit, and individualized to each student's ability. Instructional delivery provides oppor-tunity for movement and concentration, along with time devoted to repetition of activities that lead to the students' mastery and own discoveries.

Systematic Instruction. Systematic instruction refers to a set of step-by-step instructional routines that are supported by the research. These include beginning with a review, presenting in small steps, providing active practice, checking for understanding, guiding students, providing feedback, and con-tinuing to practice until students are independent (Rosenshine, 1987).

From the design of the Montessori materials to their display in the class-room, the curriculum and its associated materials are organized systematical-ly. Each area of the classroom offers materials that promote successive levels of concept development. For example, in the first section of the Language Area, the youngest students are introduced to vocabulary cards representing people, animals, and objects found in their immediate environment. There are sound games to engage students' ability to hear subtle sound differences and enhance phonological sensitivity, such as the I Spy Game, along with the use of Sound Cylinders and the Montessori Bells, all reviewed in Chapter 3. Small objects, housed in baskets or other accessible containers, support stu-dents' understanding of initial sounds. Students then move on to Sandpaper Letters to support understanding of the alphabetic principle, associating in-dividual letters with their appropriate sounds. There are pre-writing oppor-tunities using a Movable Alphabet to identify initial, end, and medial sounds of words using the prefabricated letters to then "make" or compose words. Over time, students use a smaller Movable Alphabet to construct short sto-ries, while also engaging in authentic opportunities to simultaneously build reading skills through sight word recognition, blends, digraphs, and other semantic features of our language.

Explicit Instruction. Explicit instruction can be described as a purposeful way of teaching that includes clear modeling, guided practice, and indepen-dent practice (Archer & Hughes, 2011; Rosenshine, 1987). This type of in-struction is aligned with how Montessori educators are trained to provide clear and concise lessons. Regardless of training affiliation, all Montessori educators learn the progression of each domain of the curriculum (language, math, sensorial, etc.) through demonstrations following step-by-step proce-dures required for each material designed to ensure students' success.

Research is clear that students benefit from explicit and systematic in-struction (Hattie, 2009). An observation checklist of effective instruction developed by the Texas Center for Reading and Language Art (2002) lists several indicators of explicit systematic instruction that parallel teaching practices in Montessori classrooms. For example, teachers

- Limit the amount of new information to be taught
- Model/demonstrate "think aloud" effectively
- Provide examples
- Maximize student engagement
- Pace instruction appropriately
- Check for understanding
- Reteach when necessary
- Provide corrective feedback (many of the Montessori materials do this without teacher intervention)

Many of the explicit instruction indicators are evident during a Montessori instructional strategy called the Three Period Lesson. Originally developed by Édouard Séguin (1907) as an effective method of teaching children with learning differences, Dr. Montessori adapted the three-tiered lesson strategy as an integral instructional component of the pedagogy. Lessons in Montessori classrooms often focus on one or two learning objectives. Teachers demonstrate or model how to use materials appropriately, with dedicated time in each lesson for students to replicate and practice the activity—first with support from the teacher, then on their own. During the lesson, the teacher monitors student understanding, and this, in turn, influences the instructional pace or the in-the-moment decision to reteach what the student does not yet understand. These in-the-moment formative assessments inform whether to reteach during the current lesson or to follow up on another day. Similar consideration is given to explicit feedback, often considered more developmentally appropriate for elementary (6–9, 9–12-year-old children) and beyond. An example of the Three Period Lesson using the Sandpaper Letters can be found in Chapter 4.

Personalized Instruction. Montessori education is recognized as one pedagogy that embraces many of the elements required to support personalized learning. More than an approach to differentiated instruction, personalized learning "affords the learner a degree of choice about what is learned, when it is learned, and how it is learned" (Murphy, 2016, p. ii). Further, this choice and variation enhance student motivation, fostering "self-direction and . . . mastery of knowledge and skills" (p. ii). The focus is on the student experience, so the teacher's role is as a facilitator who demonstrates learning experiences, offers feedback to students, helps learners set goals and select tasks, collaboratively designs learning assessments to evaluate performance, and serves as a mentor throughout the process (Mavrič, 2020).

In a Montessori classroom, Keefe and Jenkins's (2002) elements of personalized learning are evident. Early childhood classrooms (preschool and kindergarten) with a 3-hour uninterrupted morning work time are adhering to one component of the Montessori pedagogy with high fidelity. This dedicated work time allows children adequate opportunity to explore the carefully prepared learning environment and practice with self-chosen instructional materials within a set of expectations determined by the teacher. Additionally, they can work at their own pace, which allows students time to learn in different ways and at different rates. Learning is both an individual and social process. Assessment is authentic. Classrooms are interactive, thoughtful learning environments that reflect a culture of collegiality (Keefe & Jenkins, 2002, 451–452).

In Montessori primary grade and elementary classrooms, there are still long periods of instructional time for students to work independently, with groups, or with the teacher. Montessori elementary teachers are trained to foster a personalized learning framework that develops the students' commitment to their own mastery, goal-setting, and continuous progress. Further, in Montessori primary grade and elementary classrooms, students are taught to become increasingly independent in forming appropriate learning goals with the teacher and seeking actionable feedback from the teacher, classmates, or other resources in the classroom. These are exemplary components of goal-setting, organizing learning, self-monitoring, feedback, and mastery. Each of these components has been identified in John Hattie's synthesis of influences relating to student achievement in regard to being in the zone of desired effects (Hattie, 2009). In order to uncover those practices that work best in schools, Hattie employed statistical measures to synthesize more than 50,000 studies with more than 80 million student participants. This study resulted in his 2009 book, *Visible Learning: A Synthesis of Over 800 Meta-analyses Relating to Achievement*. It is in this work that the influences of goal-setting, organizing learning, self-monitoring, feedback, and mastery on student achievement are evidenced as well as being in the zone of desired effects. If implemented with fidelity, these practices will accelerate learning and have the possibility of resulting in progress equal to more than 1 year of growth (and even 2 or 3 years of growth) in one year's time.

Movement and Concentration. Concentration is an important element of learning, and Montessori educators design environments that promote extended opportunities for uninterrupted engagement. The American Montessori Society's AMS School Accreditation Standards & Criteria (2018) help schools define and "demonstrate the quality and integrity" of their programming. One of the nine quality standards, Standard 3: Teaching and Learning, refers to learning opportunities that optimally occur in a 3-hour uninterrupted work cycle, 5 days a week, in Early Childhood and Elementary classrooms (Standard 3.7.2 and 3.7.3). This dedicated work period, free from external interruptions, allows students time and freedom to self-select materials and to choose to work alone or with others, for as long or as short a duration as they determine within the 3-hour work period. Dr. Montessori believed concentration, this deep engagement, occurs not through children's interactions with people or abstract ideas or worksheets, but through interactions with materials designed to enhance learning. As an example, the child's movement of carrying the materials from the shelf to a work area provides a sense of weight; manipulating the materials helps the student to understand their purpose. For the youngest students, the use of the Knobbed Cylinders and Pink Tower (described earlier in this chapter) provide opportunities to experience height and width. Later, alphabet letters outlined with a fine-grained texture are physically traced by the student to encourage motor memory that is also associated with its appropriate letter sound. The order of the classroom, in combination with the order of the materials and structured delivery of instruction, all work toward providing ongoing opportunities for students to engage deeply in learning activities.

Contemporary psychologist Mihaly Csikszentmihalyi described his research of the human experience of deep engagement, or *flow*, as "you lose your sense of time . . . the idea is to be so saturated with (your task) that there's no future or past, it's just an extended present in which you're making meaning and dismantling meaning" (Csikszentmihalyi, 1996, p. 121). These words echo Dr. Montessori's own observations of children made 80 years earlier. The children in her classrooms exhibited characteristics of "absorbed attention, a profound concentration which isolates [him] from all the stimuli of his environment" (Montessori, 1916/1965, p. 218). In this state of deep concentration, motivation is intrinsic and not directed by external demands (the teacher) or requirements (the curriculum or class schedule).

To encourage flow, Csikszentmihalyi noted that one must be engaged with a task that can advance their current ability. The challenge should be neither beneath one's current skill level (resulting in boredom), nor beyond one's current ability (as the task would cause frustration rather than engagement). For educators, this translates to the importance of providing students with classroom environments that offer extended periods of time protected from interruptions as a foundation for building concentration and intrinsic motivation. This is especially important because these early experiences of concentration can support later learning. Csikszentmihalyi noted that when people were able to move easily into flow, they were also able to screen out what was irrelevant to a task, allowing them to concentrate with greater efficiency. But when some people worked harder to focus, they were less likely to attain a deep sense of engagement (Flaste, 1989).

Repetition and Discovery. E. M. Standing (1957/1998), in his biography of Dr. Montessori, described how often in education, teachers instruct their students on a particular topic and once teaching is completed, they move forward to present the next topic in the curriculum. In a Montessori classroom, however, these initial lessons are considered introductory and serve as only the first step in the learning process. Standing quotes Dr. Montessori as she reaffirms that *teaching* a skill or concept is not the same as *learning* that skill or concept. "When the child has come to understand something that is not the end, but only the beginning. For now, there comes the 'second stage' . . . the more important one, when the child goes on repeating the same exercise again and again for the sheer love of it" (p. 246). In Montessori classrooms, students have the opportunity to reinforce individualized lessons by revisiting materials as often as they are interested in doing so (freedom of choice), as well as exploring similarly designed materials that support the same learning objectives.

For example, as will be found in Chapter 7, Montessori Language materials include Classification Cards, which build children's understanding of their world through pictures, labels, and short definitions. Once a lesson has been presented, the student may return to the material to practice at any time during the 3-hour morning work period.

This same lesson can be replicated using other Classification Cards available on the Language shelf. Organized by category, images and text related to food, buildings, clothing, transportation, art, and so forth offer an infinite number of words and concepts to the child. As Montessori offers an integrated curriculum, from early childhood through elementary years and beyond, similar Classification Cards can also be found in the Sensorial, Geography, and Science areas of the classroom, offering students opportunities to explore geometric shapes, plants, land and water forms, and animals by genus and species, respectively. The topics are limited only by the interests of the child and what is known in our universe.

Culturally Responsive Pedagogy. Long before the development of contemporary frameworks that focus on linguistic and cultural diversity, Dr. Montessori encouraged the adaptation of her pedagogy to best reflect the language and culture of the students enrolled in her schools. For example, elements of Ladson-Billings's (1995) Culturally Relevant Pedagogy can be seen in Dr. Montessori's teacher training, in which she invites educators to engage in reflective protocols to examine internal beliefs and biases. And just as Moll et al.'s (1992) "funds of knowledge" value students' home and community experiences, Dr. Montessori also required educators to design learning activities that would acknowledge and further develop students' understanding of their own language and their home, community, and local environment, as well as other culturally relevant information. These cultural adaptations are most observable in the Practical Life and Language areas in early childhood classrooms. For example, early childhood Practical Life activities reflect the work that children observe their parents (or other adults) in their culture doing, allowing for variance according to the many backgrounds of children in the classroom. Students use real tools and utensils such as child-sized brooms to sweep floors, or apple slicers to cut and core apples to serve to friends.

When studying other cultures, teachers may add *ohashi* (chopsticks) to snack tables and Japanese brush painting and origami activities to extend geography lessons.

In Montessori elementary classrooms, culturally responsive practices are purposely embedded across the curriculum, consistent with Dr. Montessori's view that developmentally, elementary-aged students are uniquely sensitive to culturally responsive practices. Dr. Montessori viewed the elementary years as a sensitive period for developing a consciousness regarding our interconnectedness with people across the world and appreciation for our similarities and differences. One example of Dr. Montessori's culturally responsive view is the use of a framework to study any group of people from any time period. This framework, the Fundamental Needs of Humans (see Chapter 6), makes clear to children that all humans in all times have fundamental needs. The framework is illustrated on a chart that outlines the fundamental needs of humans as falling into two larger categories: material needs (physiological and safety) and spiritual needs (higher-level needs or wants for a happy life). The material needs are identified as shelter, food, clothing, transportation, defense, and safety, as well as communication. The spiritual needs are identified as love, religion, culture, style, and self-care. Students are led to discover and appreciate that depending on location, time in history, and access, humans meet their needs in different ways. This discovery helps them develop an understanding and respectful connection to other cultures, times in history, and their world.

The next chapter will review important elements identified as the Science of Reading.

CHAPTER 2

Science of Reading Overview

The "Science of Reading" has become a phrase that is tossed around in multiple settings, including the media, policy, and curricula. Interpretation as to what is actually meant by the "Science of Reading" frequently varies. Some incorrectly attribute the Science of Reading to be solely phonics instruction. The Science of Reading holds power, for many current instructional decisions are based on alignment to this science. With critical education policy being attributed to the Science of Reading, it is important to have a shared understanding of what this term means. No one entity offers a definitive description of this phrase, but it is generally accepted that the Science of Reading embodies the collection of neuroscience and psychology research that explores the cognitive development of reading skills. Those who align curriculum or professional development to this term are most likely building their work on the seminal reading research conducted 30 years ago and reviewed below.

In an effort to "unify all stakeholders on behalf of students to ensure the advancement of educational equity," the Reading League (2021) proposed a shared definition of the Science of Reading derived from researchers from cognitive psychology, communication sciences, education, special education, linguistics, neuroscience, and others:

> The science of reading is a vast, interdisciplinary body of scientifically-based research about reading and issues related to reading and writing. This research has been conducted over the last five decades across the world, and it is derived from thousands of studies conducted in multiple languages. The science of reading has culminated in a preponderance of evidence to inform how proficient reading and writing develop; why some have difficulty; and how we can most effectively assess and teach and, therefore, improve student outcomes through prevention of and intervention for reading difficulties. (p. 6)

In this book we, too, refer to the Science of Reading as this compendium of knowledge regarding how the brain learns to read that modern technology and research has given to us.

STRUCTURED LITERACY

The term "structured literacy" is frequently used interchangeably with "the Science of Reading." In 2016, the International Dyslexia Association introduced the term "structured literacy" in an attempt to collectively refer to the literacy practices that represented the Science of Reading. In essence, structured literacy is the Science of Reading in action. Structured literacy uses cognitive research made visible through functional magnetic resonance imaging (fMRI) brain scans to create evidence-based classroom practices. Elements of structured literacy include explicit phonics instruction delivered in a systematic and explicit manner. Particular emphasis is placed on letter-sound correspondences. Students are taught phoneme-grapheme mapping, the ability to segment words into sounds and link the alphabetic symbols that represent those sounds to write words. Morphology, the study of words, exists alongside this explicit phonics instruction and becomes increasingly important as students develop as readers.

SEMINAL RESEARCH

To provide a fuller understanding of the Science of Reading, the authors present a brief overview of three seminal documents that serve as the foundation of reading research: the National Research Council's *Preventing Reading Difficulties in Young Children* (1998); the National Reading Panel's *Teaching Children to Read* (NICHD, 2000), and the National Early Literacy Panel's *Developing Early Literacy* (2008). Because there is often a lag between research findings and their application in classrooms, these documents are important for educators to have an awareness of, as they serve as the foundation of what is today identified as the Science of Reading—and as this book will highlight, also align with the Language curriculum globally implemented in Montessori classrooms.

Preventing Reading Difficulties in Young Children (NRC, 1998). Recognizing the importance and long-term influence of reading on children's academic success, a national committee was assembled to better understand why a large number of children in the United States "do not read well enough to ensure understanding and to meet the demands of an increasingly competitive economy" (p. 1). The report summarized an overwhelming body of evidence that indicated children's early exposure to oral language and literacy skills, along with the opportunity to learn in high-quality classroom environments with well-prepared educators, placed young children at an advantage for later reading achievement. To prevent reading difficulties, the committee recognized that instruction in early elementary (1st through 3rd grade) needed to be explicit as it "directs children's attention to the sound of oral language and to the connections between speech sounds and spellings [that] assist children who have not grasped the alphabetic principle" (p. 6).

Teaching Children to Read (NICHD, 2000). Building on the National Research Council's work, the National Reading Panel (NRP) created subgroups to review an extensive list of published reading research. The report highlighted five key areas of effective reading instruction in early elementary grades, including: (a) phonemic awareness—the ability to identify the different sounds in speech; (b) phonics—the skill to match letter sounds to printed letters; (c) fluency—the ability to read accurately and quickly; (d) vocabulary—the lexicon to know and understand everything within and beyond the student's immediate world; and (e) comprehension—identifying when a student reads fluently and with a strong vocabulary and reads with understanding.

Knowing the impact good teachers have on students' academic success (Marzano et al., 2003; NICHD, 2000), teacher preparation programs must include instruction that informs how children learn to read, why some children have reading difficulties, and how to identify those difficulties using comprehensive assessment practices, as well as how to implement evidence-based instruction and intervention based on reading research.

Developing Early Literacy (NELP, 2008). The National Reading Panel (NICHD, 2000) informs policy and reading instruction once children begin their academic journey in kindergarten. However, there was a gap in knowledge regarding literacy practices prior to kindergarten. The National Early Literacy Panel (NELP, 2008) was federally convened to explore literacy development from birth through age 5. The *Developing Early Literacy* report summarized research related to young children's early literacy development, with specific attention given to the influence of home and family on children's learning. The purpose of this report was to "identify interventions, parenting activities, and instructional practices that promote the development of children's early literacy skills" (NELP, 2008, p. vi), in an effort to build kindergarten readiness.

The report concluded with 11 variables that consistently predicted later literacy achievement. Six of these variables demonstrated medium to large predictive relationships to literacy development (NELP, 2008, p. vii):

- Alphabet knowledge (AK)
- Phonological awareness (PA)
- Rapid Automatic Naming (RAN) of letters/numbers
- Rapid Automatic Naming (RAN) of objects/colors
- Writing or name-writing
- Phonological memory, the ability to remember spoken information for a short period of time

Five additional early literacy skills were also moderately associated with later literacy development. These included:

- Concepts of print—knowledge of print conventions (direction of print) and book concepts (cover, title, text)
- Print knowledge—a combination of alphabet knowledge, print concepts, and early decoding
- Reading readiness—a combination of alphabet knowledge, concepts of print, vocabulary, memory, and phonological awareness
- Oral language—vocabulary along with the ability to understand and produce spoken language
- Visual processing—the ability to match or discriminate visual symbols (NELP, 2008, p. viii)

Interventions that focused on strategies that enhanced students' understanding of the alphabetic principle by improving phonological awareness, as well as students' ability to match letter symbols to letter sounds, reported the most statistically significant impact across an array of early literacy outcomes. For example, shared book reading experiences increased both print knowledge and oral language skills, indicating there are many authentic experiences families and preschools can offer to improve young children's literacy development.

Though these foundational studies date back over 30 years, outcomes from this collective reading research continue to inform reading instruction today. Interestingly, when reviewing research published after the National Reading Panel (NICHD, 2000) and the National Early Literacy Panel (2008) reports, Brown and her colleagues (2021) at the University of Utah were not able to identify empirical studies that contradicted the reports' major findings. Instead, the articles they reviewed actually served to "bolster or expand those findings" (2021, p. 9).

These seminal studies in turn informed two reading models, the *Simple View of Reading* and *Scarborough's Reading Rope*. To help Montessori teacher preparation programs and Montessori educators, especially those working in publicly funded charter schools, the authors have aligned Montessori Language materials to this same reading research and explicitly outlined connections using Hollis Scarborough's Reading Rope as the framework for this book.

SIMPLE VIEW OF READING

The Simple View of Reading model (Figure 2.1) was first introduced by Philip Gough and William Tunmer (1986). Based on empirical research, the model describes reading comprehension as "the product of word recognition and language comprehension" (Hoover & Tunmer, 2021, p. 2).

Figure 2.1. Simple View of Reading Model

Adapted from Gough & Tunmer, 1986.

Tunmer and Gough (2021, p. 400) defined each of the three constructs in their model. *Decoding* or Word Recognition is the ability to recognize printed words accurately and quickly, and *Language Comprehension* is the ability to both extract and construct literal and inferred meaning in speech. The product of these skills leads to *Reading Comprehension*, which is the ability to extract and construct literal and inferred meaning from print. Their studies have confirmed that both components (Word Recognition and Language Comprehension) are necessary for reading success. This can be illustrated by a mathematical equation: $1 \times 1 = 1$. The equation can be read as a student who has both strong word recognition skills and strong language skills yields a student with strong reading comprehension.

However, for a student who has poor word recognition skills (such as using the first two letters of a word to guess the rest of the word), but who has strong language comprehension skills, the equation $0 \times 1 = 0$ highlights that the deficit in word recognition skills will negatively impact their reading comprehension. The inverse is also true, $1 \times 0 = 0$. A student who has strong word recognition skills but poor language comprehension (they can read the words but don't understand the meanings of the words) will also struggle with reading comprehension. A deficit in one area cannot be compensated for by the other and will ultimately negatively impact successful reading.

The Simple View of Reading helps educators and teacher educators focus on the two main components needed to ensure that all children become successful readers.

HOLLIS SCARBOROUGH'S READING ROPE

In 2001, Hollis Scarborough developed the Reading Rope diagram (Figure 2.2). The Reading Rope further explains the Simple View of Reading by outlining the discrete skills needed to be a successful reader. The Reading Rope consists of two main components: Language Comprehension and Word Recognition. Within each component are individual reading skills, referred to as "strands" of the rope, that research has identified as key skills students need to master to become competent readers.

The Word Recognition component is made up of three strands: phonological awareness, decoding, and sight word recognition. As Moats (2020)

Figure 2.2. Scarborough's Reading Rope, 2001

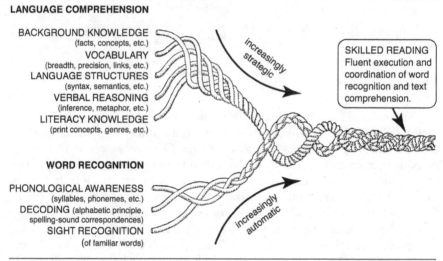

LANGUAGE COMPREHENSION

BACKGROUND KNOWLEDGE
(facts, concepts, etc.)
VOCABULARY
(breadth, precision, links, etc.)
LANGUAGE STRUCTURES
(syntax, semantics, etc.)
VERBAL REASONING
(inference, metaphor, etc.)
LITERACY KNOWLEDGE
(print concepts, genres, etc.)

increasingly strategic

SKILLED READING
Fluent execution and
coordination of word
recognition and text
comprehension.

WORD RECOGNITION

PHONOLOGICAL AWARENESS
(syllables, phonemes, etc.)
DECODING (alphabetic principle,
spelling-sound correspondences)
SIGHT RECOGNITION
(of familiar words)

increasingly automatic

Image courtesy of Guilford Press.

states, "the term 'sight words' is unfortunate, because word images are stored not by their global, visual characteristics, but by the mapped correspondences between phonemes, morphemes, and print patterns" (pp. 14–15). This process of learning words to a level of immediate recognition is referred to as "orthographic mapping" and is discussed further in Chapter 5, "Sight Recognition."

The Language Comprehension component is made up of five strands: background knowledge, language structures, vocabulary, verbal reasoning, and literacy knowledge. While the Word Recognition strands develop word automaticity and fluency, the Language Comprehension skills create strategic readers. Scarborough's Reading Rope displays the complexity of becoming a skilled reader. You will note, the image references phonics through the decoding strand, but effective reading instruction must seek to strengthen all components of the Reading Rope to foster strong reading skills.

This book has been intentionally constructed using Scarborough's Reading Rope as a framework. Part I begins with those Word Recognition skills students need to master with growing automaticity: phonological awareness, decoding, and sight recognition. Part II focuses on strategic Language Comprehension skills: background knowledge, vocabulary, language structures, verbal reasoning, and literacy knowledge. Each chapter reviews a single strand, providing the reader with a definition, relevant research, and connections to Montessori materials. Each chapter concludes with instructional strategies from conventional classrooms that align to Montessori principles and that may serve as a reference for additional evidence-based activities all educators can implement to support a range of students' learning.

CONSIDERING THE MONTESSORI CURRICULUM AND ALIGNMENT TO SCIENCE OF READING (SoR) LITERATURE

The Science of Reading principles and Montessori curriculum have much in common. First and foremost is that both are rooted in scientific research. Dr. Maria Montessori built her method on scientific research and saw this as key in addressing the issues of the day: "The basis of reform for education and society, which is a necessity of our times, must be built on scientific study" (Montessori & Joosten, 2004, p. 9). Because both are rooted in scientific research reflective of their historical era, it is not surprising that there is significant overlap in the methodologies. Both Montessori education and Science of Reading methodologies are highly multisensory, systematic, and explicit in nature. They both feature materials, instruction, and concepts that (a) follow a systematic and logical scope and sequence; (b) build from basic to more challenging in an intentional progression; (c) use step-by-step procedures and routines; (d) teach elements of a specific, targeted system (e.g., sound-to-symbol correspondence); and (e) encourage students to practice each concept to automaticity.

Explicit instruction, for the purposes of this book, refers to an "unambiguous and direct approach" that is highly structured and systematic and

> is characterized by a series of supports or scaffolds, whereby students are guided through the learning process with clear statements about the purpose and rationale for learning the new skill, clear explanations and demonstrations of the instructional target, and supported practice with feedback until independent mastery has been achieved. (Archer & Hughes, 2011, p. 1)

This type of explicit instruction and immediate corrective feedback is evident in the Science of Reading and in Montessori methodologies. What differs may be the mechanism by which they are delivered. For example, in many more conventional educational settings, feedback is generally given directly by the teacher to the student either verbally or in writing. While this can also occur in a Montessori setting, it's the very nature of the didactic Montessori materials to often contain a self-correcting feature that also offers immediate feedback to the student. Take, for example, an activity with 12 picture cards and four letters representing initial sounds. The activity is designed so that each letter sound is associated with only three picture cards. If the student finds that they have four pictures with one letter sound and only two with another letter sound, they would need to rethink their answers. Other self-correcting strategies include the use of answer keys or charts for students to self-assess their work. Whether by means of direct interaction with a teacher or with didactic materials, the salient point is that a student should not leave a lesson with a sense that an incorrect response is correct. Importantly, John Hattie's synthesis of meta-analyses of influences on student achievement has shown that the main components of explicit instruction (direct instruction, scaffolding, and teacher clarity) are in what he refers to as "the zone of desired effects," meaning that utilizing this method supports more than 1 year's growth in students in a 1-year time frame (Hattie, 2009).

Other consistencies between Montessori education and the Science of Reading include ongoing and repetitive practice, a high level of student–teacher interaction, utilization of examples, decodable books, and a loop of responsive feedback (Spear-Swerling, 2019). Examples include Dr. Montessori's emphasis on repetition as a means for children to understand, synthesize, apply, and internalize what they are learning: "Repetition is the secret of perfection" (Montessori, 1948/1967, pp. 97–98).

The next chapter will introduce the Word Recognition strands of Scarborough's Reading Rope, Montessori materials that align with these strands, and additional research-based activities to support all learners.

WORD RECOGNITION

Participants in Dr. Maria Montessori's training program attended daily sessions over 4 months that focused on either education principles and child development or lecture-demonstrations that reviewed presentations and the use of Montessori materials (Montessori, 2012). Of the 33 pedagogical sessions listed in Dr. Montessori's 1946 London lectures, more than half of them made references to aspects of language and reading development. Whether discussing the construction of man; transmitting history, science, or culture; sustaining democracy; or developing intelligence or imagination, language and reading development are themes woven throughout Dr. Montessori's work.

As discussed in Chapter 2, Hollis Scarborough's Reading Rope (2001) serves as a map noting the skills students need to practice and master to become skilled readers. The strands found within two distinct categories—reading skills associated with Word Recognition and those associated with Language Comprehension—serve as the framework for this book.

Part I highlights Montessori materials and research-based activities supporting the Word Recognition portion of Scarborough's Reading Rope, teachable skills involving a "narrow scope of knowledge (e.g., letters, sounds, words) and processes (decoding) that, once acquired, will lead to fast, accurate word recognition" (Kamhi, 2007). The strands from this section focus on (a) phonological awareness, (b) decoding, and (c) sight recognition. These three skills allow an individual to unlock a word by turning the symbols on the page into a meaningful word unit. According to Scarborough (2001), when some children struggle to learn to read, often it's an issue of not having mastery of skills identified in these Word Recognition strands.

In most Montessori classrooms, students have a 3-hour uninterrupted morning work period, allowing for ongoing opportunities to revisit activities, a practice that helps solidify mastery of new content. As a student returns to

Figure I.1. Scarborough's Reading Rope, 2001

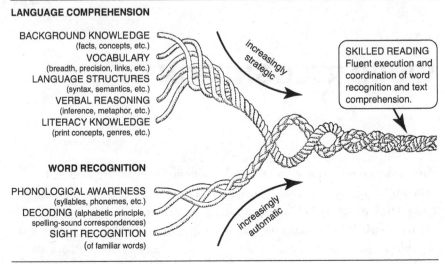

Image courtesy of Guilford Press.

practice with a specific material, the teacher is also provided with multiple observation snapshots of their students' learning over time. The Montessori word recognition lessons mirror Lerner and Lonigan's (2016) description of phonological awareness skills working in tandem with phonics skills.

Students in Montessori classrooms begin with auditory discrimination activities to build phonological awareness skills that will in turn influence later success in phonics. As students become sensitive to the sounds of their language, they can then transition to matching letter sounds to letter symbols. From here, students have ongoing opportunities to *encode* or *make words* using the Movable Alphabet. This encoding period is then followed by decoding activities as students read phonetic words, match labels to Three-Part Cards, and progress into reading definition booklets and other decodable texts. Montessori materials that support word recognition skills will be located primarily in the Language area of the classroom (e.g., Sandpaper Letters, Movable Alphabet).

Part II of this book highlights *language comprehension*, including background knowledge, vocabulary development, language structures, verbal reasoning, and literacy knowledge. Language comprehension is knowledge dependent. It requires students to have a broad understanding of content across different domains (e.g., science, history, geography). In a Montessori classroom, lessons that support language comprehension are found not only in the Language area of the classroom, but also throughout the entire curriculum. Lessons provided in language, sensorial, science, geography, botany, and other curriculum areas are paramount to supporting students' comprehension skills and will be further elaborated in each reading strand.

The next chapter provides an overview of the phonological awareness strand of Scarborough's Reading Rope. It begins with a review of current reading research, followed by Montessori lessons that align with this strand. The reader is then offered additional exemplar activities often found in conventional classrooms that may also be helpful in Montessori contexts.

CHAPTER 3

Phonological Awareness

Phonological awareness, "the appreciation of speech sounds without regard for their meaning" (National Research Council [NRC] et al., 1998, p. 248), is foundational for building students' word recognition skills. From the moment they enter the world (and even earlier), children naturally respond to environmental stimuli, which in turn influences the development of auditory milestones such as turning their head or smiling when hearing a family member's voice, recognizing words for common objects (e.g., cup, shoe), and enjoying being read to—all within their 1st year of life (Stanford Children's Health, n.d.). Research points to *sound* as a scaffold or "bootstrap" for cognitive development. Conway et al. (2009) noted that "because the brain is an integrated functional system, sensory processing . . . [is] not completely independent from the rest of neurocognition and thus may have secondary effects on the brain and cognition as a whole" (p. 275).

With this in mind, pre-reading students greatly benefit from activities that develop their phonological sensitivity. By helping students to recognize and differentiate the sounds they hear, we are scaffolding their later ability to read. Instructional time should be devoted to activities that enhance "detecting and producing rhymes and alliterative sequences in songs and speech, identifying objects in the environment whose names begin (or end) with the same sound, (and) clapping to indicate the number of syllables (or phonemes) in a spoken word" (NRC, 1998, p. 187). Phonological awareness is so important that when students enter kindergarten without these skills, they often struggle with reading difficulties (p. 248).

To be clear, phonological awareness focuses solely on sounds. When we ask students to visually recognize individual letters and letter patterns in words and connect them to letter sounds, we're now introducing the alphabetic principle. In your teaching, phonological awareness skills are fostered through the elementary grades but are most critical in early childhood.

SCIENCE OF READING—PHONOLOGICAL AWARENESS

Terminology associated with the phonological awareness strand of Scarborough's Reading Rope—phonological awareness, phonemic awareness, and phonemes—can be confusing. **Phonological awareness** serves as the umbrella term for all sound-related skills, whereas **phonemic awareness** refers to the ability to discriminate between individual speech sounds. A **phoneme** is the smallest unit of sound. **Phonological awareness** encompasses all speech sounds and includes recognition and manipulation of words, syllables, rhymes, and individual speech sounds. Since phonological awareness focuses on sounds only, students first learn to segment, delete, add, substitute, and blend sounds orally—without print. Soon after, **phonics** instruction occurs once letters are introduced along with their respective letter sounds. However, phonics is not actually part of the phonological awareness strand.

Other vocabulary associated with phonological awareness includes syllables, word parts or whole words with one voiced vowel sound. For example, the largest unit of language is a word (e.g., lighthouse), which can be broken down into smaller units, such as by syllable (light—house = two separate syllables). A **syllable** is a word part or whole word with one voiced vowel sound.

A word can also be broken down into a unit of language called **onset-rime.** For the word "pen," the onset is the first sound (or sounds) before the vowel, in this case /p/. The rime is the vowel and everything that follows. The rime for "pen" is /en/. The smallest unit of sound is the phoneme, and an important part of phonological awareness is helping children to hear each of the individual sounds in a word. There are three phonemes in the word "pen": /p/ /e/ /n/. Wordplay that is all auditory falls under this broader umbrella called phonological awareness.

Phonological awareness is foundational to reading. When students take part in ongoing structured activities that support their ability to recognize and manipulate sounds, over time it leads to associating those sounds with specific letters and letter patterns (alphabetic principle). In reading research, strong phonological awareness skills are building blocks in the literacy continuum, and the ability to isolate single phonemes within a word is crucial to both reading and writing.

Progression of Skills. When thinking of phonological awareness, it is important to keep in mind that the ultimate goal of literacy instruction is to create a reader. As stated earlier, phonological awareness activities are not taught with letters or text themselves. A student does not need to master all phonological awareness skills before learning to read. In fact, phonics instruction that links phonemes (sounds) with graphemes (letter or letter combinations) can be taught simultaneously (Brady, 2020 NICHD, 2000). Identifying words within a sentence, onset and rime, syllables within words, and individual phonemes (through blending, segmenting, and sound manipulation) are foundational phonological awareness skills that will enable a student to decode and encode words. "Integration of instruction in phoneme awareness, letter sounds and letter names supports learning of each and also contributes to the foundation for parallel processing of neurological information about letters and words that will provide the speed and robustness of decoding and word recognition as reading skills develop" (Brady, 2021, p. 1). In linking to orthography sooner rather than later, children continue to develop their blending and segmenting skills.

The following section provides examples of Montessori materials that support students' understanding of phonological awareness relating to letter sounds *without* letter symbols. The connection between letter symbols and their individual sounds is not addressed in phonological awareness activities but is detailed in the decoding strand of Scarborough's Reading Rope (2001). For phonological awareness, students enjoy sound games focusing on initial sounds as well as ending and medial sounds of words. These sound-based activities can also include segmenting words, blending sounds, and recognizing and creating rhymes. The descriptions provide the reader with an understanding of Montessori materials that build phonological sensitivity, as well as how they align to the Science of Reading. It should be noted the descriptions provide an overview of the Montessori materials and can be used to augment more comprehensive lessons learned during formal Montessori training.

PHONOLOGICAL AWARENESS IN THE MONTESSORI CLASSROOM

Dr. Montessori spoke of sensitive periods in a child's development when certain activities were more effective—what would now be termed developmentally appropriate. In a Montessori classroom, children as young as 3 years old typically begin developing phonological awareness skills through play-based small-group and individual lessons. These activities align with outcomes noted in the National Research Council's (1998) seminal study, *Preventing Reading Difficulties in Young Children,* highlighting several decades of reading research and pointing to the importance of phonological awareness skills and their influence on reading outcomes. As an example, prior to asking children to accurately identify sounds in words, such as "What is the first sound you hear in the words big, bat, and bun," the Council recommended focusing on auditory discrimination as a precursor skill by improving students' "ability to perceive other nonspeech sounds such as tones, environmental noise, music, and so forth" (NRC, 1998, p. 55).

Since phonological awareness by definition means sounds of speech—letters, syllables, and words—the focus is on listening skills with no specific printed language materials used when working with children. There are several preliminary literacy Montessori materials that support young children's auditory discrimination that in turn will support their foundational phonological awareness skills. Preliminary phonological sensitivity activities within a Montessori classroom include Sound Cylinders and the Montessori Bells, which support auditory or sound discrimination, as well as I Spy Games,

Figure 3.1. Sound Cylinders

Image courtesy of Nienhuis Montessori.

along with rhyming books and songs that can be directly linked to the discrimination of letter sounds to support early literacy development.

Sound Cylinders. The Sound Cylinders (Figure 3.1) can be found in the Sensorial area of the Montessori classroom. The cylinders are sorted into two boxes, one with a red lid and the other with a blue lid. In each box are six prefilled wooden cylinders, with each cylinder containing a different granular material that makes a different pitch and volume of sound when turned upside down and gently shaken. The contents can include sand, rice, and small bells. Sounds from cylinders in one box match the contents and sounds of the cylinders in the other box. In this auditory discrimination activity, the young child systematically matches the cylinders and then grades the matched cylinders beginning with the matching cylinders with the softest sound (sand) to the loudest sound (bells).

The Bells. Montessori Bells (Figure 3.2) are intended to train the young child's ear to recognize matching notes. The classic set consists of 16 bells on wooden bases in two matching major scale octaves. Using a wooden mallet and a damper, the child's task is to strike one bell fitted on the varnished stand and then locate the matching tone by striking a bell fitted on either a white or a black stand (similar to a piano keyboard). By helping to focus the child's attention on a single sound, this pre-literacy auditory discrimination activity can help refine children's ability to hear subtle differences in sounds in the English language, such as /m/ and /n/ or /b/ and /p/. Though both the

Figure 3.2. Montessori Bells

Image courtesy of Nienhuis Montessori.

Sound Cylinders and the Montessori Bells support pre-literacy learning, they are often found not in the Language area of the classroom, but in the Music or Sensorial area of the early childhood Montessori classroom.

I Spy Game. This activity initiates the youngest learners in a listening game that requires no special materials, yet can be implemented every morning as part of morning circle to attune children's listening skills to the sounds of words. A simple phrase, "I spy with my little eye" is said aloud to the group, readying them to listen for sound clues: "I spy with my little eye something in the room that begins with the sound /m/." While remaining at the circle/rug, the children will look about the room and excitedly call out objects they observe that begin with the letter sound (mat, marker, mop, map). When a child identifies an object that begins with a different sound—for example, the sound /n/, such as napkin—the teacher can use this as a teachable moment by saying,

> Let's see, mmm-map begins with the /m/ sound and nnnn-napkin begins with the /n/ sound. They certainly sound very similar, but look how my lips come together when I make the /m/ sound and how my lips and tongue change when I make the /n/ sound. Let's see if together we can find another word that begins with the sound /m/ in the classroom! How about mmm-mirror? Does that begin with the /m/ sound? You say the word. Yes, it does begin with the /m/ sound—well done!

Immediate corrective feedback is integral to the Science of Reading, and explicit instruction naturally occurs in this game. No connection to a letter form is made in the I Spy Game. Rather, this activity enhances children's phonological awareness, their understanding of individual phonemes (or single speech sounds) and the names of objects found within the classroom. Once children have a clear understanding of the I Spy Game, it is important to extend this activity to the final sounds of words: "I'm looking for a word that ends in the sound /t/ (paint, hat)." And finally, to the medial sound: "I'm looking for a word that has the sound /ŏ/ in the middle (log, cot)."

EXEMPLAR STRUCTURED LITERACY ACTIVITIES: PHONOLOGICAL AWARENESS

In addition to Montessori activities that support students' phonological awareness skills, additional instructional activities from conventional classrooms might be considered for adaptation in Montessori classrooms to further support learning.

Elkonin Boxes. Elkonin boxes (Figure 3.3) are also known as "sound boxes." Students, after hearing a spoken word, segment the word into separate phonemes (individual sounds), placing a token in a written box. Each box represents a separate single sound. For example, a student is given a paper with three boxes printed on it. The boxes are in a row. For each phoneme, the child moves a counter/token to each box in a left-to-right progression. "Let's say the word *cat* and move the sounds in *cat* into the boxes." Please note that at this stage the focus is on isolating the sounds and not using or referring to actual letters or spelling.

Figure 3.3. Elkonin Boxes

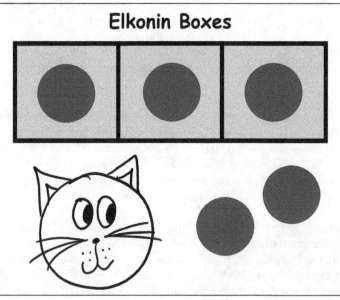

Elkonin Boxes

Figure 3.4. Elkonin Box Variations

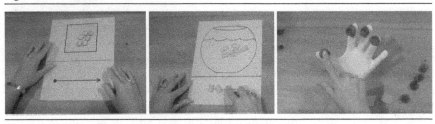

Variations on the Elkonin boxes (Figure 3.4) include moving tokens on a line that show directionality. Substituting the tokens for more tactile markers such as pom-poms is also possible. Coin collector gloves can have Velcro added to the fingertips, and students can pick up pom-poms or felt squares that represent the phonemes. Though these activities vary in materials used, they provide children with the necessary time to practice their phonological skills using different applications. Activities to support phonemic segmentation can be found at https://www.youtube.com/watch?v=dTf5gxF8-Sw.

Rhymes and Songs. Books and songs can be used with children to promote rhyme awareness. This is a wonderful and common practice in many classrooms. What is important to note is that helping children to *hear and produce rhymes* supports the auditory discrimination skills in phonological awareness. Simple nursery rhymes such as *Twinkle, Twinkle, Little Star* can be shared with young toddlers and preschoolers. There are an infinite number of songs that are just as effective for parents to sing with their children at home as they are for a teacher to sing with her class of 18 children sitting together as a whole group. Additional rhymes and songs include:

- "Head, Shoulders, Knees, and Toes"
- "Open, Shut Them"
- "Five Green and Speckled Frogs"

And books (just to name a few):

- *Sheep in a Jeep*, by Nancy Shaw
- *Jamberry*, by Bruce Degen
- *Llama Llama Red Pajama*, by Anna Dewdney
- *Giggly Wiggly: Playtime Rhymes*, by Michael Rosen, illustrated by Chris Riddell
- *Down by the Bay*, by Raffi

Phonological Awareness Curricula. Curricula such as the Heggerty series of teacher manuals provide daily phonological awareness and phonemic awareness lessons at the pre-K, kindergarten, primary, and primary extension (for grades 3–5) levels. Such lessons are designed to take approximately 10 minutes daily, and teachers can easily add them into the day either at a group or an individual level of instruction. It is also important to note that advanced phonological awareness skills continue through the upper elementary levels. *Bridge the Gap* (VanHekken et al., 2020) is a targeted intervention for 2nd grade and up, designed to enhance phonological awareness skills that may need additional instruction.

Phonological Awareness Assessment. Teachers can utilize phonological awareness assessments to determine a child's strengths and weaknesses in auditory discrimination. The CORE (Consortium on Reaching Excellence in Education) Phonological Segmentation Test offers insight into a child's understanding that sentences consist of words, that words can be divided into syllables, and that words can be separated into individual speech sounds (phonemes). The child uses hands-on manipulatives such as blocks to represent these parts of spoken language. The PAST (Phonological Awareness Skills Test) assessment developed by Dr. David Kilpatrick (2021b) delves into more complex phonological awareness skills. In this assessment, students manipulate speech sounds. They delete syllables, and they manipulate onset and rimes. In the advanced sections, students substitute individual phonemes in the initial, final, and medial placements within the word. For example, the PAST states, "Say *rift*. Now say *rift* but instead of /f/ say /s/. FEEDBACK: 'If you say *rift*, and change the /f/ to /s/, you get *wrist*; *rift-wrist*'" (Kilpatrick, 2012b, p. 241). Both the CORE and the PAST assessments are available online.

Preliminary phonological awareness activities stimulate children's sensitivity to the sounds in their language that will in turn influence their early reading skills. Training children to be cognizant of the sounds they hear sets the stage for reading. Next, the authors examine the decoding strand of Scarborough's Reading Rope, making connections between letter sounds and their respective letter symbols.

CHAPTER 4

Decoding

How exciting is that moment when a child links a sound to its representative letter! That moment when a student demonstrates one-to-one letter-sound correspondence is always cause for celebration. It is in that moment that the child moves into the area of decoding or, as it is also known, phonics.

SCIENCE OF READING—DECODING

Decoding is the ability to recognize that a letter or letters represents a phoneme (individual speech sound). The symbols or letters that represent a phoneme are referred to as *graphemes*. It is a pivotal moment in a child's early reading development when they recognize one-to-one letter-sound correspondence. And it is not long before children begin to slide (blend) these individual letters together to read three- and four-letter phonetically regular words—for example, /d/ /o/ /g/ = dog or /j/ /u/ /m/ /p/ = jump. Children then progress from knowing a letter has a single sound to understanding that certain patterns of multiple letters can also represent a single sound. For example, /sh/, a digraph that makes a single sound (phoneme), and /eigh/ in the word "weigh" also represents the single sound /ā/. Introductory phonics includes segmenting consonant-vowel-consonant (CVC) words. Students move from early decoding to decoding multisyllabic words. According to the Science of Reading, there is a specific sequence to the explicit instruction of phonics (decoding) skills, beginning with CVC words, adding digraphs and diphthongs, moving into vowel teams, and reaching multisyllabic words with the understanding of various affixes.

The Four-Part Processing Model of Word Recognition. The Four-Part Processor is a tool that illustrates how the phonological awareness strand and the decoding strand work together so that an individual can read a word. The Four-Part Processing Model (Figure 4.1) was developed by Seidenberg and McClelland (1989) to show how different areas of the left side of the brain work together to read. In the model, when an individual encounters an unknown word in their reading, the *phonological* and *orthographic* processors in the brain actively engage and work together. The *phonological processor* deals solely with sounds, addressing the speech sounds within the language. The orthographic

Figure 4.1. Four-Part Processing Model

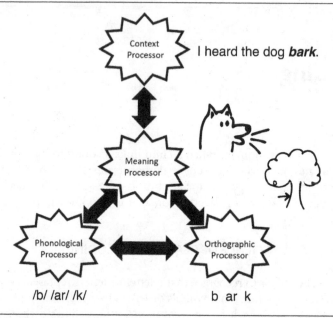

Adapted from Seidenberg and McClelland *(1989).*

processor remembers the symbols of the language; in the English alphabetic language these are the letters. The phonological and orthographic processors work together to link the sounds (phonemes) with the letters (graphemes) that they represent. This letter-sound correspondence is the heart of phonics and allows the individual to figure out what the words say by decoding the word.

At this point, the individual must now make sense of what the word means. It isn't enough to just be able to pronounce the word. The *meaning* processor links the word to previous vocabulary and background knowledge. And finally, the *context* processor determines how this vocabulary word is situated in the text considering syntax, context, and text structure.

Figure 4.1 illustrates the operation of the Four-Part Processing model with the word "bark" as read in the sentence "I heard the dog bark." First the reader recognizes the letters and recalls the phonemes that the letters represent. The meaning processor relies on the reader's vocabulary lexicon and knows that /b/ /ar/ /k/ can mean either a dog's bark or the bark of a tree. The context processor uses the sentence in which the word was read to determine which "bark" is being referred to in the given context. In actuality, these four processors operate instantaneously.

Ehri's Phase Theory. In a 2020 article published in the International Literacy Association's journal *Reading Research Quarterly*, Dr. Linnea Ehri outlined her significant body of research focused on understanding how beginners learn to read and the importance of providing them with systematic phonics instruction. Unlike her colleague Ken Goodman (1970), an early psycholinguist who offered a theory of learning to read that focused on teaching students to predict text by referring to picture or semantic cues on the page, Dr. Ehri proposed "that readers read words accurately not by guessing but by storing written words in memory and then reading them from memory by sight" (Ehri, 2020. p. S46). She proposed a continuum of four word reading phases that "reflect the predominant type of knowledge that readers apply to read and spell words" (p. 550) that included a pre-reader phase, a partial alphabetic phase, a full alphabetic phase, and the consolidated alphabetic phase. Table 4.1 provides a brief description of each of Ehri's phases and then aligns the continuum to Montessori reading instruction.

Table 4.1. Phase Theory (Ehri) Adapted to Montessori Word Reading Development

| | Phase Theory by Dr. Linnea Ehri (2020, p. 550) Adapted to Montessori Word Reading Development | | | |
	Pre-Alphabetic	Partial Alphabetic	Full Alphabetic	Consolidated Alphabetic
DEFINITION	Students know very few letter sounds and are able to read few, if any, sight words. Students tend to rely on visual or context clues but not letter-sound relationships to read and write words.	Students know most letter sounds and recognize letter-sound relationships. Can read a few words, but cannot decode new words. Students use partial letter-sound relationships to read and write.	Students enter the full alphabetic phase when they are able to decode new words. They can also make grapheme-phoneme connections within words to read and spell them from memory.	Students are readers who have accumulated spellings of many words in their lexical memory. These readers can use larger units to decode and read and write multisyllabic words. Acquisition can be from reading, but is also facilitated by explicit instruction using onset-rime, syllabic, and morphemic spelling-meaning units.

(continued)

Table 4.1. (continued)

	Pre-Alphabetic	Partial Alphabetic	Full Alphabetic	Consolidated Alphabetic
	Phase Theory by Dr. Linnea Ehri (2020, p. 550)			
	Adapted to Montessori Word Reading Development			
MONTESSORI	In this phase, students are engaged in varied preliminary lessons from the Language curriculum, such as Sound Cylinders and the Montessori Bells, to increase auditory discrimination, and lessons from the Sensorial area of the classroom to promote visual discrimination of shapes and colors that will support later recognition of letters that share similar features, such as m and n, and p, b, and d. Students also begin work with Sandpaper Letters to build understanding of letter-sound connections.	Students continue to learn all letter sounds using Sandpaper Letters, while also extending these skills using activities such as the Object Box and phonetic images focusing on initial sounds, ending sounds, and medial or vowel sounds. A good deal of time is also spent helping students "encode" words using the Movable Alphabet.	Students shift from encoding words to decoding or reading words. They no longer rely on the Movable Alphabet or may move to the small Movable Alphabet to write sentences and short stories prior to writing out their work on paper. They are introduced to digraphs and blends to build their orthographic memory. Beginning readers use decodable texts to reinforce new spelling patterns.	Continued work using Function of Words cards, sight words, labels, and story cards in the Sensorial, Science, and Cultural areas of the curriculum supports students' ability to build their lexical memory.

DECODING IN THE MONTESSORI CLASSROOM

Building on children's trained sensitivity to individual phonemes through the use of phonological awareness activities in the previous chapter, Montessori materials provide explicit connections between letter sounds and their corresponding letter symbols when working on the decoding strand. In Montessori classrooms, students have many opportunities to build a memory for shapes using Montessori materials such as the **Metal Insets**, as well as letter shapes and their associated sounds using **Sandpaper Letters**. Later, students *make words* using the **Movable Alphabet**.

In a Montessori classroom, much time is devoted to "making words" or encoding, as students convert speech to text using the Movable Alphabet (described below). To effectively decode, or read by converting print to speech, students must be able to "(1) identify the individual sounds (phonemes) in words, (2) recognize the letters as they appear in print, and (3) identify each letter's corresponding sound(s)" (Foorman et al., 2016, p. 14). The following Montessori activities support these skills.

Metal Insets. Considering Seidenberg and McClelland's (1989) Four-Part Processing Model of Word Recognition, the orthographic processor represents the work of the occipital lobe of the brain, where memory of shapes, letters, and words is reinforced. Prior to learning letter sounds and their associated shapes, students in the Montessori 3–6 classroom have many opportunities to build understanding of two- and three-dimensional shapes using Sensorial materials. The Geometric Cabinet offers six drawers containing two-dimensional shapes: Drawers 1 and 2 include circles and rectangles of varying diameters and lengths; Drawer 3 contains different triangles (acute-angled isosceles, obtuse-angled isosceles, a right-angled scalene, etc.); Drawer 4 contains polygons (pentagon, hexagon, heptagon, octagon, etc.); Drawer 5 contains quadrilaterals (rhombus, parallelogram, trapezoid, etc.); and Drawer 6 contains curved figures (ellipse, curvilinear triangle, oval, and quatrefoil). The Geometric Solids (described in Chapter 1) offer students opportunities to explore three-dimensional shapes. All of these materials support foundational math concepts, build rich vocabulary, and refine children's visual discrimination skills.

The Metal Insets (Figure 4.2) invite students to select from diverse frames (quatrefoil, oval, ellipse, curvilinear triangle, etc.) that are traced as a prewriting exercise that supports students' understanding of shapes while also developing fine motor control in preparation for using a pencil. These multisensory activities enhance students' rudimentary discrimination skills. Next, the authors will demonstrate how students progress to matching letter shapes to their respective sounds (phonemes) using Dr. Montessori's Sandpaper Letters.

Figure 4.2. Metal Insets

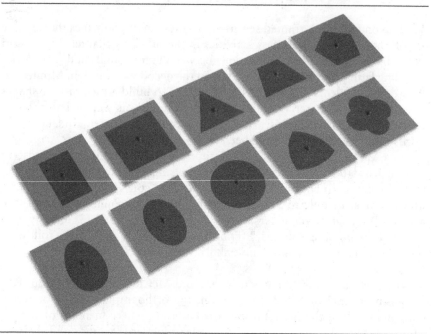

Image courtesy of Nienhuis Montessori.

Sandpaper Letters. Perhaps one of the most recognizable materials developed by Dr. Montessori, Sandpaper Letters (Figure 4.3) are individually formed letter shapes made with fine sandpaper mounted on pink tagboard, if consonants, or on blue tagboard, if vowels. Some Montessori classrooms use cursive Sandpaper Letters (Figure 4.4), which are constructed in the same format as the print version. Interestingly, some research suggests that learning to read and write using cursive supports the development of cognitive, motor, and literacy skills, and instruction in cursive handwriting has been associated with improved academic outcomes for students with identified needs, such as dyslexia (James & Atwood, 2009; Ose Askvik et al., 2020). One possibility is that to write legibly using cursive, "fine motor control is needed over fingers. You have to pay attention and you have to think about what and how you're doing it" (Klemm, 2013). Sandpaper Letters allow students to see the letter shape, to hear the sound the letter makes as the teacher says the sound aloud, and then also have the opportunity to trace the shape, integrating multiple sensory pathways to reinforce learning.

Even children as young as 2 or 3 years old who demonstrate an interest in the letters—those found in their name or words noted in a picture book—can be introduced to Sandpaper Letters. The educator selects three letter tiles to introduce to the student, making sure to not select letters with similar

Figure 4.3. Sandpaper Letters (Print)

Image courtesy of Nienhuis Montessori.

Figure 4.4. Cursive Sandpaper Letters

Image courtesy of Nienhuis Montessori.

features such as *n* and *m*, or *b* and *d*. Then, utilizing a formative assessment strategy known as the Three Period Lesson, the teacher demonstrates how to trace and say the letter sound. The three-period lesson was originally developed by Edouard Séguin, a physician who worked with children with special needs and who greatly influenced Dr. Montessori's work and the use of this strategy along with others in her method (Montessori 1948/1967).

The following provides a brief description of the Three Period Lesson in teaching a child letter-sound correspondence using Sandpaper Letters.

Three Period Lesson With Sandpaper Letters. The teacher reviews observation data to select three Sandpaper Letters a student has either not yet been introduced to or has not yet mastered the sounds that correspond to the correct letter. For the lesson, the letters m, s, and a have been selected. The teacher places the "m" sandpaper letter directly in front of her student and slowly traces the letter using their index and middle finger. Once the letter has been traced, the educator then says the letter sound aloud to the child "/m-m-m/" and then repeats the sequence once again (trace, then say letter sound).

Next, the teacher invites the child to replicate tracing and saying the letter sound aloud. The same sequence is followed for all three sandpaper letters selected for the lesson. This is the first period, or "I Do," of the lesson. If the child has successfully completed this portion of the activity and remains interested, the teacher can now move to the second period, or "We Do," of the lesson. Laying the three sandpaper letters on the table in front of them, the teacher asks:

"Which letter makes the sound /m/?"
"Point to the letter that makes the sound /s/."
"Show me the letter that makes the sound /a/."

This portion of the activity serves as an opportunity for repetition, as the teacher is responsible for saying the sounds and the child is simply pointing to the correct letter. After a few rounds of playful inquiry and if the child continues to be successful and interested, the third period, or "You Do," portion of the lesson can begin. It is now that the child is asked to identify the correct letter sound, sometimes using what's called the "Knock-Knock Game." The three sandpaper letters are turned face down on the table, the child is asked to knock on the back of one of the letters ("knock-knock"), turn it right-side up ("who's there?"), and the child is now responsible for saying the correct letter sound ("/s/").

Movable Alphabet. Once children can identify between 12 and 15 letter-sound correlations with at least two vowel sounds, they are ready to be introduced to the Movable Alphabet. The Movable Alphabet contains premade wooden or plastic letters that allow children to focus on encoding, or "making words," by listening to the individual sounds in a word and then selecting the correct letter symbol from the Movable Alphabet box to create words on a mat or table. On a shelf in the Language area, the teacher has organized a small basket containing a number of miniature objects such as a dog, a hat, a bed, a log, and a cup. To introduce the lesson, the teacher will remove the first object from the basket, look at it closely, and then name it aloud ("dog"). Next, the teacher places the dog on the top-left corner of the mat, emphasizing the first sound of the word, "/d-og, d-og/." Following this, the teacher then models locating the correct letter in the movable alphabet box, laying it carefully on the mat just to the right of the dog on the mat. The teacher repeats this sequence of steps for the remaining letter sounds to make the word "dog."

It should be noted that in the early stages of this activity, the child is not asked to read the word. Rather, the focus is on encoding or building words. After a few weeks of using the material, moving from a box of phonetic objects to phonetic pictures, the child will often begin to read the words on their own. Once a child is reading the words they have made, an extension of this

Figure 4.5. Movable Alphabet

Image courtesy of Central Montessori Academy.

work could include asking the child if they would like to write their words on paper. These writing opportunities serve as extensions to the word-building (encoding) and word-reading (decoding) activities, providing students with authentic practice opportunities to master newly developed skills.

The Movable Alphabet also supports early writing through invented spelling opportunities (Figure 4.5). "Beginning writing with invented spelling can be helpful for developing understanding of phoneme identity, phoneme segmentation, and sound-spelling relationships" (NRC, 1998, p. 195). There is much to be learned in viewing students' early writing attempts with the Movable Alphabet. A student who uses the Movable Alphabet to write "*I luv is crem*" for "I love ice cream" has demonstrated their ability to identify certain vowel and consonant sounds—as well as provided evidence for future lessons in vowel pairs (/ea/ to spell *cream* instead of *crem*) or silent -e (to spell *ice* instead of *is*). Later, during instruction in early elementary grades, there is explicit instruction on *correct* or conventional word spelling, as well as practice opportunities that lead students to have more confidence in their spelling.

Phonological Awareness Continuum to Inform Movable Alphabet and Word Work Lessons. To support Montessori educators in creating evidence-based word building extensions, the phonological awareness continuum can be extended to inform a progression for Movable Alphabet lessons outlined in the next section.

As stated earlier, phonological awareness instruction should work in tandem with children's understanding of letters (orthographic development). Contemporary reading research supports the Montessori approach, noting that phonics instruction should move from decoding tasks that are easier, such as decoding single syllables, to those that are more difficult, such as complex letter patterns (Brady, 2020). The following outlines extension lessons for Movable Alphabet.

Using a Continuum of Phonological Awareness Skills for Movable Alphabet Extension Lessons. The Movable Alphabet is a box containing 26 wooden letters. Consonants are in red, and vowels are blue. As described earlier, the prefabricated letters are used to "make words" that represent the individual phonemes students hear when sounding out phonetic words (e.g., cat, log). Small objects or picture cards can also be included with each activity. The following sequence can serve as extensions of the Movable Alphabet work to offer students the repetition needed to strengthen grapheme-phoneme connections by **isolating** initial, end, and medial sounds; **adding** sounds to words to create new words; **segmenting and blending** phonemes; **deleting** initial and ending phonemes; and **substituting** phonemes.

Isolation. Ask students to identify particular sounds (initial, end, or medial) from each word. Objects in small basket can include: dog, pan, mop, cat, lid, pen, mug, etc. During initial lessons, (1) focus on just one isolated sound (e.g., only initial sounds) and (2) remove only those letters from the Movable Alphabet box needed for the lesson. Using the objects listed above, for the initial sounds activity, retrieve d, p, m, c, l, p, and m; for end sounds, retrieve g, n, p, t, d, n, and g; and for medial sounds, retrieve o, a, o, a, i, e, u.

- *Initial sounds*—"This is a pan. Can you place the pan on the mat and say the word?"

   "What is the first sound in pan? Can you find the letter that makes the sound /p/ and place it beside the pan?"

   Repeat the lesson in this way for all of the objects.
- *End sounds*—On another day after the child has demonstrated an understanding of initial sounds, repeat the lesson in a similar format but now isolate another sound in the word. For example, "This is a mug. Can you place the mug on the mat and say the word?"

   "What is the last sound in mug? Can you find the letter that makes the sound /g/ and place it beside the mug?"
- *Medial sounds*—And on another day, isolate the medial (vowel) sound. "This is a lid. Can you place the lid on the mat and say the word?"

   "What is the middle sound in lid? Can you find the letter that makes the sound /i/ and place it beside the lid?"

Addition. Build words using similar rimes, sometimes known as word families, and differing onsets (e.g., rime: at; hat, bat, sat). During initial lessons, remove only those letters required for the lesson from the Movable Alphabet box. In this example remove several /a/ and /t/ letters from the box, along with the initial sounds planned to make each word.

Example: *"Today we're going to make words that end with the sound /at/. The first sound is /ă/ and the second sound is /t/."* Teacher demonstrates by placing letters from the Movable Alphabet onto the mat one at a time, saying the sound of each letter.

- *"Now I'm going to change the word to /pat/. The first sound is /p/."* Retrieve the /p/ and place it on the mat.
- Repeat the first sound and say the second sound: *"/p/-/ă/, the next sound is /ă/."* Retrieve the /a/ and place it beside the /p/ on the mat.
- Repeat the first and second sound, then say the third sound: *"/p/—/a/—/t/, the next sound is /t/."* Retrieve the /t/ and place beside the /a/ on the mat.

These early activities with the Movable Alphabet help children to encode or sound out the words; therefore, they are not asked to read or decode the words. Decoding can happen after several weeks of short encoding lessons and may happen spontaneously as children's automaticity with sound-grapheme skills increases.

As students gain mastery of three- and four-letter phonetic words, this lesson can be expanded to create greater orthographic connections to words that have different spelling patterns, such as: /ight/, /oon/, /ay/, and /aw/.

Segmenting and Blending. When the child has increased automaticity in phoneme-grapheme skills, use the Movable Alphabet and phonetic picture cards to place individual sounds through a segmenting exercise, and then combine them or blend the sounds to read the word. In this stage children move from encoding (making words) to decoding (reading words).

- *"This is a picture of a dog. Let's place the letters that make the word dog next to the picture."*
- Place the picture on the mat, and then, working with the child, place the letters on the mat, sounding out each one /d/—/ŏ/—/g/ (segmenting, or sounding out each of the letter sounds in the word).
- Now, sliding your index finger under each letter, ask the child, *"What word did you make? /d/—/o/—/g/ You made the word /dog/"* (blending, or sliding the sounds together, to read the word).

Deletion. Make a series of words on a mat using the Movable Alphabet, removing either the initial or end sound to create a new word:

- Delete <u>initial</u> phoneme lesson. Words to make using Movable Alphabet: farm, spark, spill, start, spot.
  - » *"Let's read the first word together, /farm/. If I take away the first sound /f/, now what is the word?"* (arm)
  - » *"Could you read the next word, please? That's right, /spark/. If you take away /s/, what word is left?"* (park).

- Delete **final** phoneme lesson. Words to make using Movable Alphabet: start, pant, dogs, etc.
  - » *"Let's read the first word together, /start/. If I take away the last sound /t/, now what is the word?"* (star).
  - » *"Could you read the next word, please? That's right, /pant/. If you take away /t/, what word is left?"* (pan).

Substitution. Make a series of words on a mat using the Movable Alphabet. Students are asked to remove a letter and replace with another to create a new word:

- *"Let's read the first word together, /king/. If I substitute the first sound /k/ for /s/, now what is the word?"* (sing)
- *"Could you read the next word, please? That's right, /teach/. If you substitute the /t/ for /b/, what new word have you made?"* (beach).

EXEMPLAR STRUCTURED LITERACY ACTIVITIES: DECODING

Building on the SoR phonological awareness activities described in the previous chapter, the student transitions from working solely with phonemes (sounds) and activities such as finger-spelling and blending to now attaching the letters (graphemes) that represent those sounds. Similar to work with the Montessori Movable Alphabet, consensus in reading research points to the use of tactile letters to manipulate during instruction as a powerful tool for improving reading outcomes (Brown et al., 2021; NELP, 2008; NICHD, 2000).

There are numerous additional resources for educators to consider when teaching decoding lessons:

Word Chaining. Manipulating one letter at a time, students can create words that build off of each other. This activity is frequently referred to as *word chaining* and can be done with any letter manipulatives such as magnetic letters or letter cards. Cookie sheets work well for displaying magnetic letters, and many phonics curricula provide some type of letter manipulative. Word chaining activities can be found online and should be selected to practice the phonics skill being learned. Only one letter should be changed at a time. The terminology "word-building" may be used for this activity also. The Axelson Academy's "Manipulating Sounds: Word Building" video at https://www.youtube.com/watch?v=LNOqu6QcUwI (Axelson Academy) is another source of information.

For example, use the letters to make the word "cat." Change a letter to make the word "mat." Change a letter to make "mat" become "map." Change another letter to make the word "mop." The progression of difficulty would be to first work with initial letters, then final letters, and finally medial letters.

Many SoR curricula incorporate word-building activities into their daily lesson plans. For example, Fundations (Wilson, 2012), a Tier 1 structured literacy curriculum that addresses foundational reading skills for grades K to 3, comes with a magnetic board and letters for each student to use in creating and manipulating words. The teacher uses index-sized letter cards to build words on the whiteboard at the front of the class. Fundations also provides magnets with diphthongs, digraphs, and "glued sounds" such as "ing" and "ong."

Decodable Readers. Decodable readers are a key addition to the Structured Literacy classroom. Decodable readers are short books and/or passages that allow students to practice their newly learned phonics skills within a connected text. *Bob Books* (Maslen & Maslen, 2006) are a wonderful first-reader set, as they provide students with the opportunity to practice decoding CVC words. Unlike other "early reader" materials, decodable text is a phonetic text. For example, if a child has recently learned that "sh" makes the /sh/ sound, a decodable text that supports this skill will have numerous "sh" digraphs throughout the book. Students repeatedly get to apply this phonics rule. This following is a list of decodable texts. The list is not exhaustive, but it provides a good starting place for teachers who are building a classroom library reflective of the Science of Reading.

All About Reading
Bob Books
Bonnie Kline Passages (Language Circle)
Dog on a Log Books
EPS Phonics Plus Readers
Flyleaf Emergent Readers
Flyleaf Decodable Literature Library
Go Phonics Readers
Heggerty Decodables: Frog Series and Toucan Series
High Noon Dandelion Launchers
Little Learners Love Literacy
Miss Rhonda's Readers
Primary Phonics Storybook Sets
Spaulding Readers
S.P.I.R.E. Decodable Readers
Voyager Sopris Power Readers

The Science of Reading has shifted the mainstream classroom away from predictable texts. In the past, children might have read a book titled *Ice Cream* with a text such as "I want ice cream. The pig wants ice cream. The dog wants ice cream. The mom wants ice cream." Picture clues supported students' guesses as to the word that changed on each page. A story such as this is referred to a "predictable text." In the Science of Reading, we move away from external cueing systems such as looking at the pictures, looking at just the first letter of a word, or guessing what word would make sense. Instead, children are instructed to decode words by attending to all the letters in the word. Therefore, decodable texts become crucial to reading instruction. This does not necessarily mean all leveled texts should be removed from the classroom. Leveled texts may be repurposed to build background knowledge or inferencing skills.

Isolated phonics instruction is not the goal of the SoR. Phonics instruction is always brought back to how that skill translates into actual reading or writing and decodable texts allow skill practice to be applied in connected text.

Phoneme-Grapheme Mapping. An effective strategy to teach the encoding of words, phoneme-grapheme mapping supports students in learning phonics rules and then applying this new knowledge through structured word building. Students are given a grid paper. In an activity much like Elkonin boxes, children begin by moving a token for each phoneme they hear in the word into a box. Then, through direct instruction of particular phonics skills, students replace each token with the letter or letters that create that single sound (Figure 4.6). Note that more than one letter can be in a box. It is the grapheme (the letter or letter combinations) that make up that sound as written. Each box is one phoneme (sound).

The Reading Rockets website offers easily accessible information about phonics and decoding activities and can be accessed at https://www.readingrockets.org/reading-101-guide-parents/first-grade/phonics-and-decoding-activities-your-first-grader.

Decoding instruction continues into the upper grades as students learn more complex phoneme-grapheme connections and explore the etymology of words and how the word's origin affects its alphabetic spelling.

While decoding is a key strand within the Word Recognition component, keep in mind that the strands are never taught in isolation. At the same time strong phonics skills are taught, so is the development of vocabulary and comprehension. As exemplified earlier in the Reading Rope, it is the combination of reading skills that produces a successful reader.

Figure 4.6. Phoneme-Grapheme Mapping

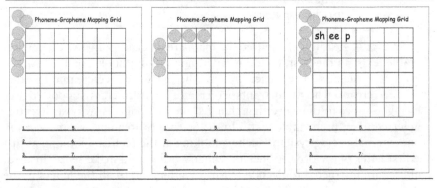

CHAPTER 5

Sight Recognition

Fluent readers can find pleasure in reading, as they do not have to sound out the separate phonemes of each word in text they read. Their fluency allows them to automatically recognize these words, thus freeing the reader to focus on the meaning behind the words. This chapter considers the skills needed for our students to demonstrate similar fluency through sight recognition.

SCIENCE OF READING—SIGHT RECOGNITION

The Science of Reading has brought to light a new definition of what comprises a "sight word." In the 1970s and '80s, sight words were defined as words that did not follow typical English language patterns; specifically, they didn't fit the patterns delineated in the six syllable types. Words such as *the, what, come,* and *from* were identified as sight words. Because these words didn't "follow the rules," teachers were trained to tell students they would just have to memorize those words in a "whole word" approach to learning. Placing these words on flashcards was common practice. Then students would drill those flashcards. Parents would diligently quiz their children using word cards sent home for additional practice. Teachers would construct Word Walls highlighting these words in the classroom. These practices were put in place as strategies to promote frequent visual exposure to sight words as a way to help students visually recall the list of words.

With the Science of Reading came the understanding that orthographic mapping, the instantaneous recognition of words and word parts, enables immediate word recognition (Kilpatrick, 2021a; Stone, 2020). This knowledge has resulted in a revision to what is meant by a sight word. The term "sight word" should apply to any word that a reader instantly recognizes and identifies without conscious effort. A fluent reader recognizes most words in a split second (research says in less than 1/20th of a second), and all of those instantly known words are sight words.

The nomenclature of "familiar" or "known" words more accurately describes the understanding of this group of words as seen through the lens of Scarborough's Reading Rope. Words known on sight include both high-frequency words and less frequently used words. A fluent reader has between

30,000 and 60,000 words in their sight word vocabulary (Sedita, 2020), and each person's sight word lexicon is unique. A musician may have a word such as *cacophony* in their lexicon, and a doctor may have *obdormition* or *xerosis* in their sight word vocabulary.

There can be no question that a proficient reader's fluency, their ability to accurately decode text with prosody at a speed that does not hinder higher-level thinking skills, is absolutely necessary in order to be an expert reader. "Automatic word recognition, which is dependent on phonic knowledge, allows the reader to attend to meaning; likewise, slow, belabored decoding overloads short-term memory and impedes comprehension" (Moats, 1998). Readers demonstrate their underlying knowledge of orthographic and morphemic structures when they decode nonsense words. The ability to apply knowledge of language structures and patterns in new situations demonstrates the deeply mapped organization of the English language. Thus, assessments that include nonsense words (e.g., DIBELS's Nonsense Word Fluency Assessment; Read Naturally's Quick Phonics Screener) illuminate the orthographic mapping that exists and areas where automaticity of specific structures must be built.

SIGHT RECOGNITION IN THE MONTESSORI CLASSROOM

Dr. Montessori focused on providing young children with encoding activities, opportunities to compose or "make words" with the Movable Alphabet prior to their learning to decode, or read words. In effect, children enrolled in Montessori classrooms first learn to write as the pathway to reading (Montessori, 1965). With this in mind, a student's first experience with irregular words occurs when encoding words with the Movable Alphabet. Dr. Montessori was aware that some languages, like Italian, were phonetic and therefore easier to learn, while nonphonetic languages such as English have a great many phonetic inconsistencies. Dr. Montessori indicated that "the teacher can compose separate words with a movable alphabet, and then pronounce them, letting the child repeat by himself the exercise of arranging and re-reading them" (Montessori, 1965), allowing students needed time to revisit and repeat language and literacy activities to promote successful reading.

Recognizing that the Montessori method needed to provide guidance for teaching reading and writing to English-speaking children, Muriel Dwyer developed (with Dr. Montessori's son, Mario Montessori) an approach that works with languages with a complex orthography, such as English. This was incredibly important, as learning to read in Italian is much less complex than English due to the Italian language's much higher phonetic consistency, meaning that words are written the way they sound when spoken. As you can imagine, learning pronunciation is always much easier in phonetic languages than in nonphonetic languages. The first version of this work was developed in the 1960s, more than a decade after Dr. Maria Montessori's death in 1952. The approach is contained in the framework that is outlined in *A Key to Writing and Reading for English* (Dwyer, 1970). In this framework, the concept of "puzzle words" (words with irregular spellings that are not purely phonetic) is introduced. These "puzzle words" are then written or printed on cards that can be used with the classic Three Period Lesson (described also in Chapter 4). For example, in the first period of the lesson, the teacher reads each of the puzzle words (e.g., that, them, this), explaining that the letters /t/ and /h/ make a new sound when placed adjacent to each other, /th/. In the second period, the teacher continues to read each puzzle word, but now the student is responsible for pointing to and identifying the correct word card. And in the third period of the lesson, the student is now solely responsible for decoding or reading the puzzle words.

Given contemporary research related to how the brain orthographically maps words, this is one area of instruction that may need additional consideration. Rather than having students memorize puzzle words, research suggests educators help students identify parts of the word that are decodable, and then present lessons about any parts of a word that are not yet known. For example, to successfully read the word "other," students would need to know the sounds made by the letter /o/, and the two digraphs /th/ and /er/. When students understand that digraphs are two letters that when placed adjacent to each other make a new sound, these phonetic inconsistencies become teachable skills that will promote additional sight word recognition (e.g., brother, mother).

In a Montessori classroom, Phonogram Booklets and Phonogram Cards support students' sight recognition by highlighting in red specific letters that share a similar rule in the language being studied. Phonogram Booklets highlight in red the same letter combination on every page, while Phonogram Cards also highlight in red the same letter combination to be learned, but only within the first word at the top of the card (Figure 5.1).

Phonogram Cards reinforce students' understanding of **digraphs,** two letters that when placed together make a new phoneme (/sh/ as in ship); **trigraphs,** three letters that when placed together make a new phoneme (/tch/ as in match); and **dipthongs,** or gliding vowel sounds made when two vowels are placed together (/oy/ as in boy). There are also Phonogram Cards that reinforce **consonant blends** (/sl/ as in slip) and **long-vowel sounds** (/ay/ as in stay, /eigh/ as in sleigh, and /a_e/ as in tape—words that all make the long-vowel sound /ā/ using very different letter combinations).

The authors recommend adopting an instructional approach that focuses first on known phonemes in a word and then providing additional instruction for those parts of the word not yet known. An example of this can be found in the next section in this chapter, "Exemplar Structured Literacy Activities: Sight Recognition"—see Heart Words.

Figure 5.1. Phonogram Cards

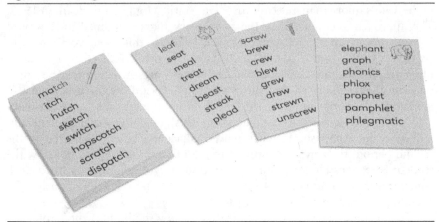

Image courtesy of Nienhuis Montessori.

These reading activities, while a part of the decoding strand, also lead to numerous exposures. Multiple exposures to content in a Montessori classroom are inherent to the design of the pedagogy. The integrated curriculum offers students literacy opportunities beyond the Language materials, within the math, sensorial, geography, and botany lessons of the curriculum. The three-hour work period provides students ample opportunity to revisit previously offered lessons, so as to practice new concepts to mastery. These multiple exposures then map the word orthographically so the word can be instantaneously retrieved in future encounters.

EXEMPLAR STRUCTURED LITERACY ACTIVITIES: SIGHT RECOGNITION

The question becomes: With the Science of Reading and our knowledge of orthographic mapping, what should be done with those words that are irregular?

The truth is, in almost all words there is at least a part of the word that does follow a phonetic rule. Only 4% of words in English are truly irregular. About 50% are completely decodable (Moats & Tolman, 2019). The rest contain decodable parts. For example, with the word "what," the "wh" is pronounced as expected, the /wh/ sound. The "t" makes the expected /t/ sound. It is only the letter "a" that surprises the readers by making a /u/ sound. A word becomes part of one's sight word vocabulary when it is decoded multiple times and orthographically mapped on the brain. Usually, teachers begin with more common words, usually referenced as high-frequency words, the words found most often in printed text. It makes sense to begin with these words, as this group of words unlocks much of the text young students will encounter.

Heart Words. Instead of memorizing the entire word through a visual memory approach, teachers should draw attention to the part(s) of the word that are decodable. Really Great Reading offers a learning sequence called "Heart Word Magic" (www.reallygreatreading.com). In this approach, students look at high-frequency words that are not easily decodable. The teacher points out the phonetically regular parts of the word, and then they help the student "highlight the tricky to make it sticky." Really Great Reading labels these words as heart words.

A word cannot become a known word unless it has been encountered at least once and for most people multiple times. The majority of people need between 4 and 30 (Sedita, 2022) exposures to a new word in order to store that word for instantaneous retrieval. A strong understanding of phonemic segmentation and the letter-sound correspondences is crucial for orthographic mapping. Therefore, activities that support these skills, phonemic segmentation and decoding, are used in the Science of Reading classroom. Thinking back to our chapter on phonological awareness, activities for phonemic segmentation include Elkonin boxes and their variations as well as finger segmenting. Focus on phoneme-grapheme mapping builds the letter-sound correspondence and will facilitate a growing number of words recognized on sight.

Decodable Readers. As discussed in the last chapter, the use of decodable readers allows students to apply phonics skills to connected text rather than learn those skills in a "stand-alone fashion." The process of orthographic mapping, the repeated recognition of a word or language pattern to map it into memory, also supports the use of decodable readers. The repetition of phonetically regular words and word parts builds automaticity for reading. In the future, when students encounter a grapheme they have repeatedly seen and decoded, they will instantly recognize it. The Science of Reading classroom will provide the opportunities for students to practice word recognition through multiple exposures, and decodable books afford students the opportunity for repeated practice of specific phonics skills.

Multisyllabic Words. Another strategy that aids in orthographic mapping is the "peeling off" strategy. Students are taught to identify and remove affixes from a multisyllabic word until they are left with the root word. The small morphological units of affixes are fixed in the brain when they are encountered again and again through this process. When decoding multisyllabic words in the future, students will recognize these word parts instantly.

Phoneme-Grapheme Mapping. While phoneme-grapheme mapping builds phonics skills in general, lessons that focus on a selected grapheme provide the multiple exposures necessary for orthographic mapping to occur. The repetition of linking a sound to its grapheme that occurs when a child practices a distinct phonics pattern is exactly what makes that language pattern memorable. The redundancy of reading and writing graphemes that is provided by phoneme-grapheme mapping makes it ideal for spelling instruction. Historically, students were pre-tested on a word list and post-tested on that same word list at the end of the school week on Friday. Teachers despaired that their students did not apply spelling knowledge to classwork. By substituting a formalized phoneme-grapheme mapping sequence, the phonetic English language is mapped and then retrievable for future use (Moats, 2022). A resource such as *Phonics and Spelling Through Phoneme-Grapheme Mapping* by Kathryn Grace (2007) is invaluable. This process allows written words that are unknown to be stored into one's "memory bank." Those words are then stored for future use and retrieved when needed during a reading task. If a student is having difficulty remembering the word (or word part), most likely the word has not yet been orthographically mapped. That mapping is necessary before a word can be successfully stored and automatically retrieved.

With a strong bank of known words, the cognitive workload switches from decoding to comprehension. A child can put their effort into thinking about what the text means instead of all their energy being funneled into figuring out what the word is. When thinking back to the four-part processor, first the word must be decoded before it enters the meaning and context processors. As students develop strong word recognition skills, language comprehension becomes the stronger predictor of reading comprehension (Cain, 2021). A list of patterns to review with students was provided by the Institute of Education Sciences (IES) 2016 publication *Foundational Skills to Support Reading for Understanding in Kindergarten Through 3rd Grade* (see Table 5.1).

PART I CONCLUSION

The authors have discussed and provided instructional examples of practices from both Montessori education and the Science of Reading within the Word Recognition strands of Scarborough's Reading Rope. This included an overview of Dr. Montessori's didactic materials and activities that instruct the skills noted in the following strands: phonological awareness, decoding (phonics), and sight word recognition within the Language area of the classroom. These chapters drew attention to the many Montessori practices that reflect the Science of Reading. Additionally, it is known that Dr. Montessori had a heart to address the needs of children. Her philosophy of education reflected her desire that all individuals should have equitable access to the

Table 5.1. Spelling Patterns

	INSTRUCTION	Examples
Consonant patterns	**Consonant digraphs** and **trigraphs** (multi-letter combinations that stand for one phoneme)	th, sh, ch, ph, ng, tch, dge
	Blends (two or more consecutive consonants that retain their individual sounds)	scr, st, cl, fr
	Silent-letter combinations (two letters; one represents the phoneme, and the other is not pronounced)	kn, wr, gn, rh, mb
Vowel Patterns	**Vowel teams** (a combination of two, three, or four letters standing for a single vowel sound)	ae, oo, oa, igh, eigh
	Vowel diphthongs (complex speech sounds or glides that begin with one vowel and gradually change to another vowel within the same syllable)	oi, ou
	R-controlled vowels or **bossy r's** (vowels making a unique sound when followed by r)	ar, er, ir, or, ur
	Long e	ee, ie, ea, e_e, ey, ei, y
	Long a	a_e, ai, ay, a_y, ei, ea, ey
Syllable-construction patterns	**Closed Syllables** (a short vowel spelled with a single vowel letter and ending in one or more consonants)	in-sect stu-dent
	VCe (a long vowel spelled with one vowel + one consonant + silent)	com-pete base-ball
	Open syllables (ending with a long vowel sound, spelled with a single vowel letter)	pro-gram tor-na-do
	Vowel team (multiple letters spelling the vowel)	train-er neigh-bor-hood
	Vowel-r (vowel pronunciation changing before /r/)	char-ter cir-cus
	Consonant-le (unaccented final syllable containing a consonant before l followed by a silent e)	drib-ble puz-zle

Foorman et al., 2016, p. 25.

world around them, access that is unlocked through learning. With an outlook toward education such as Dr. Montessori's, it is the authors' belief that Dr. Montessori would have continued to research her own pedagogy to further refine her practices, and we have also been open to new research and evidence-based activities that could further support students' literacy growth. The evidence-based activities the authors have recorded should be considered as the Montessori teacher seeks to meld current structured literacy practices within the Montessori classroom.

It is an incorrect assumption that the Science of Reading consists only of the Word Recognition strands of Scarborough's Reading Rope. To stop here would be of great detriment to students. While the foundational skills of Part I unlock the words on the page, as shown in the Simple View of Reading, reading is more than just word identification. The second component of Scarborough's Reading Rope, Language Comprehension, addresses skills that are taught to unlock the meaning embedded in the text. These skills, or strands, of the Reading Rope—background knowledge, vocabulary, language structures, verbal reasoning, and literacy knowledge—will be discussed next in Part II, as well as the Montessori materials that align to reading research and additional learning activities that can supplement classroom instruction. It is also a misconception that this strand is taught only after word recognition skills are mastered. All skills must be simultaneously a part of the students' education.

LANGUAGE COMPREHENSION

In Part II, the authors highlight Montessori materials that support the Language Comprehension strands of the Reading Rope (2001), including lessons focused on background knowledge, vocabulary development, language structure, verbal reasoning, and literacy knowledge (Figure II.1). Throughout the classroom environment, students access nomenclature cards providing accurate vocabulary reflecting the people, activities, and relevant objects to first understand their own culture and community, and then extend this knowledge by exploring other cultures across the globe. These are often referred to as *cultural lessons*, activities that invite students to build both background knowledge and rich vocabulary in geography, history, general science, botany, zoology, music, and art. For example, moving from concrete to abstract learning, the youngest students in early childhood classrooms interact with objects and picture cards depicting landforms such as an island, lake, strait, or isthmus; match flags to maps of countries around the world; and match images of flowers, leaf shapes, or various objects found in a kitchen. Older students in elementary classrooms extend this information into reading, thinking, and writing activities that include work with Dr. Montessori's Great Lessons, dramatic retellings of world events, that inspire deeper thinking about our place in the world through the aforementioned content and subject areas. Montessori teachers give five Great Lessons, which are told in a dramatic story format, feature visual aids, and include science presentations. These lessons are exciting to primary children, who have vivid imaginations and deep curiosity. The Great Lessons are about the origins of the universe and earth, life-forms coming to the earth, early humans, how writing began, and how math began.

Historically, Dr. Montessori fled Italy to escape Mussolini's regime. As is with culturally sustaining pedagogy, which calls for education that sustains diverse cultural practices to meaningfully honor all cultures and

Figure II.1. Scarborough's Reading Rope, 2001
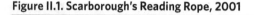

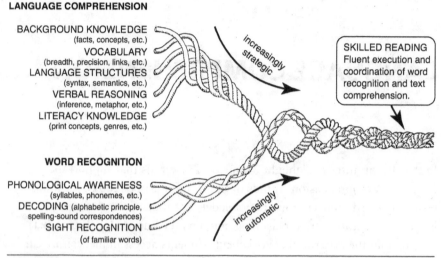

LANGUAGE COMPREHENSION

BACKGROUND KNOWLEDGE
(facts, concepts, etc.)
VOCABULARY
(breadth, precision, links, etc.)
LANGUAGE STRUCTURES
(syntax, semantics, etc.)
VERBAL REASONING
(inference, metaphor, etc.)
LITERACY KNOWLEDGE
(print concepts, genres, etc.)

increasingly strategic

SKILLED READING
Fluent execution and coordination of word recognition and text comprehension.

WORD RECOGNITION

PHONOLOGICAL AWARENESS
(syllables, phonemes, etc.)
DECODING (alphabetic principle, spelling-sound correspondences)
SIGHT RECOGNITION
(of familiar words)

increasingly automatic

Courtesy of Guilford Press.

make our schools and world more just and equitable (Paris & Alim, 2017), Dr. Montessori believed the Montessori pedagogy was a tool for justice, radical acceptance, and peace. The cultural materials described above are not isolated or separate social studies or science curriculum, but rather represent Dr. Montessori's integrated approach to culturally sustaining pedagogy that also builds language comprehension, as well as the human citizen:

> We must take man himself, take him with patience and confidence, across all the planes of education. We must put everything before him, the school, culture, religion, the world itself. We must help him to develop within himself that which will make him capable of understanding. It is not merely words; it is a labour of education. This will be a preparation for peace—for peace cannot exist without justice and without men endowed with a strong personality and a strong conscience. (Montessori, 1947/2019, p. 38).

It is the authors' hope that a clear demonstration of Dr. Montessori's vision to develop peaceful, intelligent, and thoughtful youth will be visible in the upcoming comprehension strand.

CHAPTER 6

Background Knowledge

It is important that the reader has noticed that the process of learning to read in a Montessori classroom is so much more than decoding skills (phonological awareness, knowledge of letters and sounds, and phonics). The research is clear that instruction must include all of the strands from Scarborough's Reading Rope (2001) if students are to become competent readers.

In a statement released by the Knowledge Matters Campaign Scientific Advisory Committee (2022), "sense-making requires knowledge that must be systematically built (not just activated!) through instructional experiences and curricula that evoke curiosity and the desire to learn more." Not surprisingly, students are more engaged learners when they have access to rich learning experiences, and there's no age restriction to this work. Knowledge-building should be a key component of all Pre-K–12 instruction and is

> "particularly critical for children who have inequitable opportunities to gain it. All students have knowledge and other assets that educators must value, understand, and build upon. But they also have a right to an education that builds new knowledge, addresses their instructional strengths and needs, and offers opportunities to apply their knowledge in ways that have meaning for them and their communities." (Knowledge Matters Campaign Scientific Advisory Committee, 2022)

Knowledge of the world allows all learners, young and old, to situate new learning in their minds. By linking what has been read to our prior experience and understanding, one develops a deeper understanding of what the text means. Rosenblatt's (1978) seminal Reader-Response Theory is based on the fact that the readers' personal experiences and prior understandings influence how a given text is interpreted. In essence, the text and the reader contribute equally to understanding what the words ultimately mean. A transaction takes place between the lived experience and the written word, creating a unique understanding or level of comprehension of what is written on the page.

SCIENCE OF READING—BACKGROUND KNOWLEDGE

Knowledge of our world and facts and concepts surrounding areas such as the sciences, history, geography, the arts, and the humanities is paramount in language comprehension. The reader brings their *background knowledge,* all they know of the world, to the task of reading (Smith et al., 2021, p. 216). As children have new experiences and learn new concepts or words, the information is initially stored as working memory, a component of one's executive function that supports learning. This temporary storage system then transfers the new knowledge to a child's long-term memory, cataloging their experiences with classroom instruction, media, or more direct types of lived experiences (Moats & Tolman, 2019; Smith et al., 2021). According to Scarborough's Reading Rope (2001), Word Recognition strands and Language Comprehension strands work together in an iterative fashion in a child's development of skilled reading and text comprehension. When considering the Language Comprehension strands, Scarborough noted that text comprehension will not be strong if a child does not have the critical background knowledge needed to understand the text.

This relationship between knowledge and reading comprehension suggests that our students are already at either an advantage or a disadvantage based on what they come to school knowing (Moats & Tolman, 2019). To illustrate this relationship, consider a well-known 1988 study where researchers asked middle school students to read about an inning in a baseball game and then re-create it with wooden baseball figures. The researchers found that successfully re-creating the baseball inning as detailed in the supplied reading was reflective of a student's knowledge of baseball, not of their actual reading ability. Further, weaker readers performed just as well as strong readers if they had knowledge of the sport (Recht & Leslie, 1988). Without the advantage of background knowledge from indirect or direct experience, even the most skilled readers must work and use considerable cognitive resources to make sense of text in an unfamiliar subject.

Background knowledge in a specific area allows children to process and remember related information more efficiently and to integrate newer pieces of information in that area more easily (Schneider et al., 1989). When a reader has solid background knowledge, they are able to make more connections and engage in the reading task without rereading or pausing to make connections and make sense of the ideas on the page (Willingham, 2006). This decreased cognitive load allows the reader to more simply activate connections and add layers of new information to their existing knowledge base (Miller & Keenan, 2009).

Put simply, background knowledge makes reading and learning easier. The cumulative and exponential nature of one's background knowledge can serve as a contributor to the *Matthew effect,* in which the proverbial rich get richer and the poor get poorer. In other words, the larger one's knowledge base, the more efficient and expedient they will be in acquiring a greater level and depth of knowledge (Stanovich, 1986). Similarly, the more limited one's knowledge base is, the more they will struggle to acquire a greater level and depth of knowledge. It should be noted that if misapplied, this information could contribute to a deficit narrative. Instead, the focus for all educators is to consider the importance of background knowledge to design opportunities for experiential learning and to link texts to children's lives.

BACKGROUND KNOWLEDGE IN THE MONTESSORI CLASSROOM

In the previous section, we reviewed research highlighting the importance of background knowledge as a key predictor of reading success, but given the diverse experiences children have in building world knowledge prior to entering school, it's important to consider the breadth and depth of intentional content shared with children from birth through early elementary years. A critical review of reading research (Smith et al., 2021) found that

> higher levels of background knowledge enable children to better comprehend a text. Readers who have a strong knowledge of a particular topic, both in terms of quantity and quality of knowledge, are more able to comprehend a text than a similarly cohesive text for which they lack background knowledge. (p. 226)

This holds true for both beginner readers and more skilled readers—background knowledge supports understanding when reading about that topic in text. In Montessori classrooms, beginning with the youngest learner in infant and toddler classrooms through early childhood, elementary classrooms, and beyond, building children's background knowledge is a key consideration of the Montessori Language curriculum as well as that of the cultural areas.

This section will review language materials in Montessori classrooms that support the development of children's background knowledge that begins as a pre-reading activity and builds in complexity as children become more skillful readers.

Nomenclature Cards. One hallmark of Montessori instruction is that it follows a progression moving *from the concrete to the abstract* in support of developing children's background knowledge. Concrete instruction requires teachers to share real materials that students can interact with prior to introducing a new topic or unit of study. As an example, a teacher may bring a betta fish or a parakeet or a guinea pig into the classroom. More than just class pets, they become models for learning about fish, birds, and mammals. Montessori materials include descriptions of animal habitats, how they raise their young, and what types of food they eat. Later instruction may be represented more abstractly, such as by pictures of animals or through short stories and songs shared with students to extend their understanding of the topic. Table 6.1 provides an instructional progression of a science topic to provide background knowledge about reptiles.

This same progression of concrete to abstract is applied throughout the curriculum, with materials prepared to build background knowledge and vocabulary related to zoology, geography, botany, geometry, and the categorization

Table 6.1. Material Progression from Concrete to Abstract

Example: Early Childhood Science (Zoology) Classification of Animals—Reptiles—Turtle	
Instruction aligned to concrete examples of content. Introduce turtle to classroom.	• Children observe a turtle now living in an aquarium habitat in the classroom. Their observations lead them to, draw, write, and discuss their wonderings or questions about turtles. • The children learn about and take part in the turtle's care, feeding schedule, upkeep of tank, etc.
Instruction moves to depictions of real animals and objects, to representative objects.	• Children learn about the life cycle of the turtle. Small objects representing each milestone of a turtle's development from egg to hatchling to juvenile to adult turtle allow children opportunities to manipulate, explore, and learn the proper terminology associated with the life of a turtle.
Instruction shifts to abstract materials, such as picture cards with high-quality images labeled with correct terminology.	• Nomenclature Cards or Three-Part Cards are found throughout the Montessori classroom. The structure of the cards remains the same: one card contains a high-quality image, another card contains the label used to identify the image, and the third card contains both the high-quality image and the picture label. Examples can be found in Chapter 7, Table 7.1 • Pre-readers match the images. Emergent readers match picture cards and then add matching labels. • Children extend this work by reproducing three-part picture cards, creating their own booklets, coloring and labeling the parts of the turtle's body (e.g., carapace, head, tail).
Build vocabulary and background knowledge.	• Definition Cards provide brief descriptions of each of the labels, and provide beginning readers with short text to decode, so as to learn about the turtle. • Booklets extend definitions with additional information and relevant vocabulary about turtles through accessible short text to offer readers additional opportunity to practice reading. • Nonfiction trade books and children's picture books are added to classroom bookshelves to further support and extend learning.

of objects within the child's home, school, and community environment. Additional examples are provided in the next chapter focusing on the vocabulary strand of the Reading Rope.

In the elementary classroom, background knowledge gained in early childhood is expanded upon with a curriculum that captures children's imaginations and connects them to their world. Some hallmarks of the 6–9 curriculum include stories that introduce early elementary students to their universe, life on earth, and human development on the planet, as well as stories related to written language and numbers. The cultural lessons provide historical context for students while also making explicit connections to their relevance in the child's current life. For example, the Story of Writing explores the transition from an oral tradition of language to early written alphabets so that people could express their ideas and messages using a shared written language.

Timeline of Life. Students develop an understanding of the history of the universe and all its life-forms, including glacial events, through a chart called the *Timeline of Life* (Figure 6.1 and Figure 6.2). This comprehensive timeline begins in the Cambrian Period and culminates with the Cenozoic Era. Each line of lineage traces the originating events and major extinction events of many phyla and species.

The Fundamental Needs of Humans. The Fundamental Needs of Humans is a chart material that supports students' understanding of how to study humans across time and cultures. It helps students visualize that people everywhere have the same basic needs. What varies is not the needs themselves, but the ways various cultures meet those needs. This framework empowers young learners to study any culture in current contexts as well as at any time in history. These studies provide students with an understanding that all people have fundamental needs and affords them, from a young age, the opportunity to build a thoughtful, knowledgeable, and healthy respect for all people.

Dr. Montessori viewed these lessons and activities as more than building knowledge for the sake of learning facts and constructs. She further thought that it was the role of the teacher to present these subjects, "so as to touch the

Figure 6.1. Timeline of Life

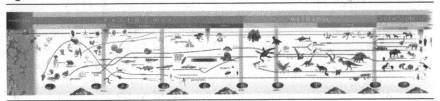

Figure 6.2. Elementary Student using Timeline of Life

imagination of the child, and make him enthusiastic, and then add fuel to the burning fire that has been lit" (Montessori, 1985, p.15).

EXEMPLAR STRUCTURED LITERACY ACTIVITIES: BACKGROUND KNOWLEDGE

Other instructional activities to consider in Montessori classrooms may include the following.

Oral Language. Oral language is considered to be a major predictor of student achievement through 3rd grade (Hart & Risley, 1995; Suskind, 2015; Walker et al., 1994). One powerful strategy is the utilization of intentional vocabulary instruction that is well-integrated with classroom learning content and that supports young children's ability to communicate their thinking (Massaro, 2015). This type of instruction can greatly contribute to a student's expanding background knowledge.

Knowledge Rich Curriculum. Thematic units should be rich in knowledge, with meaningful subthemes. As an example, Project Ready!, an open-resource curriculum, features a "Kindness Unit" with a meaningful subtheme focused on kindness to animals that includes a pretend veterinarian's office in the classroom so that children can practice being kind to animals while learning rich background knowledge about what a veterinarian does and how they care for animals. In most cases, content should be introduced in a large group and reinforced in small groups and follow-up activities (Murdoch et al., 2021).

Delivering Content. For younger elementary students, content is ideally delivered by units that are segmented into lessons in which students have booklets that are rich with illustrations and that contain minimal text as appropriate for these students' ability to decode. The teacher will deliver content that is above the reading level of most students so that the students can focus on content rather than the reading task. Any text in the students' booklets prompts knowledge-sharing between students and between students and their teachers and parents.

The focus should be squarely on building students' understanding and knowledge of the science contained in the unit, and as such, the content of a lesson should be delivered by the teacher with visual aids (Hirsch & Wright, 2004). Years of educational and cognitive research have demonstrated that listening comprehension outpaces reading comprehension from a student's early childhood years through, at a minimum, the primary grades.

To build background knowledge, teachers need to implement lessons that capitalize on young children's ability to listen to and talk about much more complex concepts than they can independently read about (Fisher & Frey, 2014). One recommended resource is the science units from Core Knowledge. which are designed to support student knowledge-building of science concepts (Hirsch & Wright, 2004).

Timelines. Timelines are commonly seen in schools as displays on walls that are only viewed by students or used as visual aids. By utilizing learning activities with interactive timeline materials, students will be able to track important events within a period of history or social construct. One recommended resource is the timeline cards contained in the Core Knowledge History and Geography program, which is designed to support student knowledge-building in history and geography (Hirsch & Wright, 2004).

K-W-L Charts. These graphic organizers have been popular in the past and track what a student knows (K), wants to know (W), and has learned (L) about a topic (Figure 6.3). These organizers are used before, during, and after instruction. The charts can help students access background knowledge, formulate what they hope to learn, and identify what information they can add to their knowledge base. Teachers using the K-W-L strategy should note that the "W," what the student **wants** to learn, does not always match the information provided in the text and may not be helpful in goal-setting or retrieval of background knowledge. For example, suppose a student is going to read a text about lions. They activate prior knowledge by listing what they

Figure 6.3. K-W-L Chart

K-W-L Chart		
K What I Know	**W** What I Want to Know	**L** What I Learned

already know about lions. Then they list what they want to learn about lions. The child may state they wish to know what lions eat. This sets a purpose for reading, but as the child reads, the text may never give this information. The time spent on the "W" is not purposeful in activating prior knowledge or meeting comprehension objectives. For that reason, a modified version of the K-W-L chart, is recommended for the "W" portion of the K-W-L for the teacher provides three things students will want to look for in the article. Utilizing graphic organizers can aid students in adopting a framework for building their growing schema and knowledge structures. Schema maps differentiate what is already known about a topic from newly learned information. In essence, the child uses their background knowledge as a link to new knowledge. Students link what they know to new pieces of information.

Primary and elementary traditional instruction may seek to activate knowledge in some of the following ways.

Anticipation Guides. The use of an anticipation guide before reading may strategically activate prior knowledge. An *anticipation guide* sets a purpose for reading while the child accesses what they already know about the topic. This pre-reading activity has students agree or disagree with a handful of statements. A skillfully crafted anticipation guide may spark discussion both before and after the text reading. For example, the anticipation guide may ask students to agree or disagree with the statement "Breathing under water is impossible." Students would draw on the fact that they know they cannot breathe under water. Some students may incorporate the knowledge that fish breathe underwater in a different manner than humans. The use of scuba gear could support being able to breathe underwater. Students would then read

Table 6.2. Semantic Feature Analysis

Semantic Feature Analysis		
Characteristics	Penguins	Chickens
Have beaks	X	X
Swim	X	
Fly long distances		
Have feathers	X	X
Eat fish	X	
Eat seed		X
Have webbed feet	X	X

the text to see what the author has to offer that might influence their understanding of this statement.

Semantic Feature Analysis (Anders & Bos, 1986; Vacca et al., 2021)—The Semantic Feature Analysis (Figure 6.2) allows students to compare the characteristics of two or more items using a grid. At the top of this grid are the items being compared. Down the left side is a list of characteristics. Before reading, students determine which of the items has the specified characteristics.

Then, after reading, students go back and can revise their thoughts regarding the attributes listed. Students activate prior knowledge and read with a purpose when using this strategy. In the younger grades, teachers may have a discussion that centers on characteristics and attributes of the focus of the reading without writing down on a formal chart. Most frequently this is a strategy that is used in specific content areas.

Activating prior knowledge should not take a significant amount of time in a lesson. Link the topic to what the child knows and then get to the reading. If necessary, provide background information necessary for the comprehension of a text. The ultimate goal is to connect to what is already stored in the brain and then to begin the reading.

Rich real-life experiences are invaluable. How fortunate are the children who enter school with a memory filled with experiential learning. All is not lost if the child has limited background knowledge. The purposeful building of vicarious experiences provides context for future reading. I have never been to outer space, but I have plenty of background knowledge about the planets and moon provided in elementary school.

CHAPTER 7

Vocabulary

Background knowledge and vocabulary are inextricably linked and provide authentic instructional opportunities to build students' knowledge of the world, while simultaneously offering the correct terminology or vocabulary that aligns to their new knowledge. Students may be taught to decode letters on a page, but they must also have the decoded word as part of their own lexicon if they are read with comprehension.

SCIENCE OF READING—VOCABULARY

Vocabulary learning is cumulative, and in an effort to support children's reading proficiency by 3rd grade, a sensitivity to word learning must be established early (Biemiller & Slonim, 2001; Hart & Risley, 1995). Of interest to those engaged in education policy related to K–12 outcomes, results of Stanovich's (1986) research noted that children who had higher-quality early learning experiences (a) acquired greater vocabulary knowledge, (b) became proficient readers, and (c) also learned more efficiently in other academic domains. This reciprocal response between vocabulary development and academic learning is labeled the Matthew effect ("the rich get richer and the poor get poorer"). It highlights how language-rich environments—homes and schools filled with conversation, book reading, and novel experiences such as visiting the local zoo, park, or children's museum—in turn influence growth in background knowledge and vocabulary (Walberg & Tsai, 1983). Unfortunately, the opposite also holds true. Children with fewer language and literacy experiences have a reduced cumulative vocabulary over time.

In the seminal study conducted by Betty Hart and Todd Risley (1995), children's vocabulary development was examined between birth and their 4th birthday. Researchers visited families in their homes to record conversational exchanges, categorizing results according to three income levels: professional families, working-class families, and low-income families who received state subsidies. In their sample, children from professional families heard on average slightly over 2,000 words an hour, whereas children from working-class households heard approximately 1,200 words and children from low-income families heard only 600 words within the same time frame. With fewer book reading opportunities, fewer instances of adults labeling or naming objects, shorter sustained conversations, and less frequent opportunities for children to express and expand on their questions and ideas, over time this correlated to a substantial word deficit and learning gap *before* a child entered their first day of kindergarten (Hart & Risley, 1995; McLoyd & Purtell, 2008). For those educators working in underresourced communities, particular attention must be devoted to designing language-building learning opportunities.

The authors share this study but offer caveats to its interpretation. Bahena (2016), in her review of critiques of Hart and Risley's methodology, presented insight regarding the study's internal validity of selected vocabulary measures and its sampling, as well as cultural blind spots influencing how data were coded and conclusions were determined. And Romeo and her colleagues (2018) remind their readers that socioeconomic status (SES) is a very broad category that can include determinants based on "income, educational access, other environmental resources, stress, health, and nutrition" (p. 701), all possible variables that might influence children's learning and development.

Follow-up studies to Hart and Risley's research continue to offer evidence pointing to the critical importance of early language exposure on children's vocabulary development (Romeo et al., 2018). Subsequent studies that collected more comprehensive literacy data and used less intrusive recording devices (Gilkerson et al., 2017) continued to highlight a family's income as a variable that can substantially influence the variation in the amount of language heard by young children. In *Preventing Reading Difficulties in Young Children* (1998), the authors highlighted the importance of "quantity" of language experiences as a variable in children's vocabulary learning:

> It's now clear that though poor and uneducated families provide much of the same array of language experiences as middle-class educated families, the quantity of verbal interaction they tend to provide is much less . . . because vocabulary is associated with reading outcomes, it seems likely that reduced opportunities for verbal interactions would function as a risk factor. (p. 122)

Further implications are important to consider, as a reduced exposure to early language and literacy experiences can inhibit acceleration of word learning strategies, and create a gap in phonological awareness skills, as well as influence limited development in background knowledge (Golinkoff et al., 2018; Neuman, 2021)—all skills critical to ensuring reading proficiency.

It is of the upmost importance that educators and those working with young children keep in mind this body of research concerning vocabulary development and recognize, respect, and build on the language(s) and cultural competence young children bring to their learning.

VOCABULARY IN A MONTESSORI CLASSROOM

In a Montessori classroom, vocabulary learning can be thought of as *strategic integrated instruction* blending both literacy and content areas. Hwang et al. (2021) define integrated instruction as a classroom practice "in which literacy activities (reading and/or writing) serve as a tool to cultivate content knowledge (science and/or social studies) while, at the same time, content teaching serves as a lever to facilitate literacy skills (vocabulary and/or comprehension)" (p. 2). Importantly, in Montessori classrooms, every child (regardless of their reading ability) has access to demonstrations, discussions, and experiences with vocabulary materials.

Classification Cards. In the previous chapter, the authors explored how background knowledge is introduced and reinforced through the progressive design of the Montessori curriculum moving from concrete representations, such as using real objects, to abstract materials such as pictures to support students' learning. In addition to building background knowledge, these materials simultaneously influence children's vocabulary development. Classification is a cognitive action "in which objects and events are grouped according to the logical relations governing their similarity" (Tzuriel et al., 2017, p. 108). Due to the seemingly infinite number of words or concepts that can be introduced to students about their world, it's best to organize objects, persons, places, or events to improve students' ability to manage and retain new words when presented in logically related categories.

In the Language area of the classroom, Classification Cards are offered as an introductory activity to build young children's vocabulary. The collections of images help children classify their world by matching images while simultaneously learning the correct terminology. Classification Cards are also referred to as Three-Part Cards because of their design: one card with a labeled image, another with just the image, and the third card that contains just the label.

The categories for Classification Cards are bound only by the objects found in one's own culture and setting. For example, one set of Classification Cards may include 10 pairs of cards with images representing objects found in a kitchen (refrigerator, plate, sink), a living room (sofa, lamp, rug), and a classroom (clock, pencil, easel). The youngest of toddlers can take part in discussions about the objects with their teacher as they match the images on a mat. Preschoolers, working on their own or with a peer, can match the images and extend the activity by then matching the label card. In a Montessori classroom, language materials are embedded throughout the curriculum. Table 7.1 provides an overview of types of Classification Cards found throughout the Montessori curriculum, including zoology, botany, geography, and music.

Table 7.1. Types of Classification Cards

Vocabulary building lessons

A collection of 10–15 picture cards, all images are related to a single topic (transportation, objects in a kitchen, playground, etc.). There are two matching images, one image that is labeled, a second image with no label, and a separate label card. These are called **Three-Part Cards**.

Below are some examples of Classification Cards found in different areas of study in the Montessori classroom.

	Classification Cards			
	Zoology	**Botany**	**Geography**	**Music**
Topic	Mammals	Leaf Shapes	Land & Water Forms	Instruments
Vocabulary *each word has its own picture card	Camel Cow Dog Donkey Goat Horse Pig Rabbit Sheep	Cordate Elliptical Hastate Lanceolate Obcordate Obovate Reniform Runcinate	Bay Cape Gulf Island Isthmus Lake Peninsula Strait	Bass clarinet Cello Drum Flute Guitar Harp Horn Piano Trumpet
Image and Label	camel	reniform	bay	guitar
Image				
Label	camel	reniform	bay	guitar

Morphology. Morphology is the study of the internal structure of words. Morphemes are defined as the smallest units of meaning (e.g., prefixes, suffixes, and base words). In Montessori elementary classrooms, lessons with morphemes are a part of the Word Study set of lessons, which includes compound words, suffixes, prefixes, antonyms, synonyms, homophones, homonyms, and homographs. Each of these morphemes is presented with an introductory key experience and follow-up lessons.

As an example, synonyms are introduced orally and using an image of two items that represent the idea of two items in which one has the power, but the other, while not as powerful, fulfills an important role—for example, a picture of a tractor and a cart. (This can be adapted using more familiar examples, such as a locomotive and a boxcar.) The teacher would first show children the picture of the tractor and explain what it does. There should be an emphasis on the fact that a tractor is powerful so that it can go through the field and do its job. Next, the teacher would show the children a picture of a cart. Then the teacher would explain that the cart can be attached to the tractor to help the tractor pull things. The teacher would then ask the children if the cart is able to move by itself, reinforcing the idea that the cart has a very important job but it cannot move without the tractor. The teacher would then show a picture of the tractor and the cart attached together, explaining to the children that they move together and that the tractor's job becomes related to the cart.

The teacher would then ask the children where they would find a tractor, ask them what they know about a farm, and show them a card labeled with the word "farm." (This could and may be needed to be adjusted to a more familiar noun and suffix, for example, engine and engineer for use with locomotive and boxcar.) Next, the teacher would ask the children who works on a farm, to which the students would reply, "farmers," The teacher would then place a card with the suffix "er" next to the word "farm." The teacher would then explain that a suffix has been added to the word "farm" to tell us who farms and that the suffix "er" is like the cart in that it has a specific job. She would also explain that when one looks up the suffix "er" in the dictionary, one definition tells us that it is added to nouns to mean someone who does the job associated with the noun. A farmer does the work on a farm. The teacher would then explain that suffixes are attached to the end of root words to add something new to the meaning of the root word.

Discussions about different suffixes with teacher direction and support would continue. Once the teacher assesses that their students are ready, the teacher would introduce them to an activity that allows students to practice with the concept of suffixes by building their own words with preselected root words and one suffix at a time, gradually building up to a number of choices of suffixes to which the student would need to find the most logical fit for each root word. Last, students would have explicit instruction in spelling rules for suffixes.

EXEMPLAR STRUCTURED LITERACY ACTIVITIES: VOCABULARY

Within the contemporary general education classroom, the Science of Reading emphasizes that vocabulary develops from three specific areas: direct instruction, self-taught words, and a literacy-rich environment. In the early grades, students need to learn approximately 3,000 words per year, and certainly those 3,000 words cannot be all directly instructed by the classroom teacher. As our previous chapter discussed, the general world knowledge of a child leads to an expanded vocabulary. A child who has visited the beach and participated in casual talk about waves, seashells, fish, and sandcastles nestles these words in their prior knowledge and is ready to relate these words to vocabulary around the beach in their later reading. However, a literacy-rich environment is not limited to experiential learning.

Children listening to spoken language is key to a literacy-rich environment. The classroom should be filled with authentic opportunities to build receptive and expressive language skills. **Receptive vocabulary**, those words students recognize, can be further developed by narration. Sandra Wilborn (2020), a literacy expert with Reading Rockets, suggests that adults can narrate their actions. For example, the teacher can demonstrate how to paint a picture of a flower by modeling their actions and while also providing rich language input describing what they are doing or thinking: "Which flower shall I paint this morning? There are three flowers in the vase, a sunflower, a chrysanthemum, and a daffodil. I'll choose the daffodil because it has such a vibrant shade of yellow." The teacher offered the proper names (sunflower, chrysanthemum, daffodil) and a word less frequently used in conversation (vibrant). Children can build their vocabulary through these contextualized learning opportunities. Although it might seem unnatural to narrate one's actions for more reticent talkers and may appear silly to onlookers, it is this stream-of-consciousness talk that provides a strong receptive vocabulary for children.

In their white paper *Young Children Develop in an Environment of Relationships*, members of the National Scientific Council on the Developing Child (2004) describe the importance of adults engaging in "serve-and-return" interactions with young children (p. 2) to foster **expressive (or speaking) vocabulary**. Human beings are not hard-wired for reading; it is a skill to be learned. Humans are, however, hard-wired for language development. Even the youngest infant "naturally reaches out for interactions through babbling, facial expressions, and gestures" (p. 2), and when the adult responds similarly to the child, it "builds and strengthens brain architecture" (p. 2). So important are these opportunities for students to hear contextualized language and to engage in conversational turns, researchers noted that,

> Neuroimaging revealed a neural mechanism by which language experience may influence brain development; namely, children who experienced more

conversational turns exhibited greater activation in left inferior frontal regions (Broca's area) during language processing, which explained nearly half the relationship between children's language exposure and verbal abilities. (Romeo et al., 2018, p. 706)

Direct instruction is an important piece of Scarborough's Reading Rope. The Science of Reading directs teachers to instruct words that are integral to understanding the text, but are not explicitly taught in the text itself. If the author provides enough explanation of the word, the student can learn the word from the reading alone. For example, "The garden was full of lupines, tall purple flowers that waved in the breeze and smelled wonderful." The child can figure out that the lupine is a purple flower from this sentence alone, and that word does not need direct teaching. Teachers strategically select words that are essential to understanding the passage and are linked to lesson objectives.

Isabel Beck and her colleagues (2015) classify words into three tiers. Tier 1 words are used in everyday language and in general do not need to be formally taught. This tier includes words like cat, house, eat, and jump. Tier 2 words frequently hold more than one meaning and are useful in many subject areas. Tier 3 words are specific to a certain area of expertise. "Adaptation" is a Tier 2 word: it can be used in many possible ways, but students probably don't hear it a lot in general conversations. "Staccato" is a Tier 3 word because it is specific to music. Tier 2 words are often chosen for direct instruction because they increase the ability to understand many types of texts. It is important that definitions are given to children in an accurate and succinct manner. Prompts such as "Does anyone know what _____ means?" open up the possibility that incorrect meanings will be given. Inevitably one or more students will remember this incorrect definition. Teachers should make sure that the students are hearing the definition as it should be remembered. Anita Archer is the master of direct instruction using vocabulary. She and her colleague Charles Hughes (2011) clearly outline the definition and then provide multiple opportunities for students to use the word. This is managed during a short instructional time span of 5–10 minutes.

Frayer Model. Specific vocabulary is also successfully taught using strategies such as the Frayer model (1969). The Frayer model (see Figure 7.1) consists of four boxes, with the vocabulary word at the center. Students fill in the four quadrants with the definition of the word, the characteristics of the word (what attributes are specific to the word), and examples and non-examples of the word. It is this juxtaposition of what the word is and what the word is not that situates the new learning in the student's mind and links it to prior learning.

The Frayer model is used most successfully with concept words and words that are more general in nature. For example, using the word "dinosaur" in the Frayer model works well. Students can give lots of examples and

Figure 7.1. Frayer Model

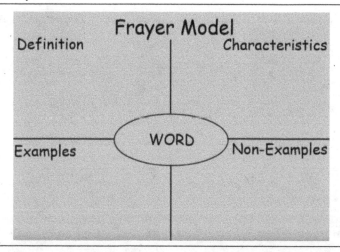

non-examples of dinosaurs. Using the word "tyrannosaurus" in the center of the Frayer model is problematic, as there is only the t-rex that is an example. Teachers should complete the Frayer model themselves before using it with students to ensure it is the best method of instruction.

   Morphology. The final way vocabulary is learned is that the words are self-taught by the student. Strategies that enable the student to grow their own lexicon are invaluable. The Science of Reading places emphasis on morphology, with a morpheme being the smallest unit of meaning. If students understand the use and meaning of affixes, roots, and inflectional endings, they can make meaning of unknown words on their own. Such understanding is called morphological awareness. Just as we manipulate individual sounds in words to build phonemic awareness, in the Science of Reading younger students are taught to manipulate morphemes to change word meaning. For example, students tie and untie their shoes. They zip and unzip their coats. They make equal and unequal piles of LEGOs. When asked to dress the teddy bear and undress the teddy bear, the child recognizes the opposite nature of the word and how the prefix "un" has influenced the meaning of the root word. And just the small number of inflections and affixes shown here (Figure 7.2) can allow students to further expand their vocabulary to make meaning of many new words.
   The Common Core Standards first begin to address morphological units in kindergarten, and Structured Literacy layers morphology into its scope of skills at the earliest stages, too. Common Core Standard L.K.1c states that kindergarten students will show mastery of forming regular plural nouns orally by adding /s/ or /es/. At the earliest stages this is done through

Figure 7.2. Inflections and Affixes to Build Vocabulary

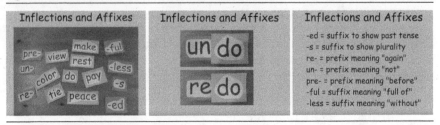

Figure 7.3. Creating Plural Words

modeling. General phonemic awareness skills state that if a word ends in a "hissing sound" (/s/, /ch/, /sh/, /x/, or /z/) you add /es/. Students can practice listening for the ending sound and adding /s/ or /es/. Figure 7.3 provides some examples.

The importance of vocabulary in reading comprehension cannot be emphasized enough. While informal assessments of vocabulary provide insight into students' mental lexicon of words, assessments such as the Peabody Picture Vocabulary Test (PPVT), a standardized assessment tool measuring receptive vocabulary, may be helpful in providing formal documentation of vocabulary skill. The assessment is typically implemented by a school's reading specialist or a special educator trained in the use of the tool. Results are reviewed with the classroom teacher to determine if additional supports or interventions are needed to improve students' receptive vocabulary.

In Chapter 8, "Language Structures," we look at the importance of the student understanding the conventions of the English language.

Language Structures

SCIENCE OF READING—LANGUAGE STRUCTURES

Language structures refer to the grammatical patterns of a language. Thornbury defined grammar as "a description of the rules for forming sentences, including an account of the meanings that these forms convey" (1999, p. 13). Some readers of this text will be old enough to remember going through specific textbooks focused on grammar alone. Some will remember diagramming sentences during their junior high school years. As more implicit methods of teaching became more pervasive in schools, the explicit teaching of grammar and language structures became less common. Educators and researchers became concerned that direct grammar teaching strategies in language structures might negatively impact students' love of reading and creative writing skills.

This concern is inconsistent with the significant research that upholds the importance of explicit instruction (Hattie, 2009). As such, the concern is for students to read sentences with accuracy and fluency; then the instructional strategies employed should explicitly teach all aspects of grammar. According to a blog post from Timothy Shanahan, "Studies over the years have shown a clear relationship between syntactic or grammatical sophistication and reading comprehension; that is, as students learn to employ more complex sentences in their oral and written language, their ability to make sense of what they read increases, too" (Shanahan, 2022, para. 1). As an example, in a quantile multiple regression analysis, researchers studied the following language factors: vocabulary, grammar, higher-level language ability, word reading, working memory, and reading comprehension and their relationships with reading comprehension. Grammar was found to be the most closely related to reading comprehension. The researchers theorize that this may be due to how grammar extends beyond understanding single sentences and affords readers the opportunity to integrate comprehension across sentences and consider the whole of the written piece (Language and Reading Research Consortium & Logan, 2017).

The relationship, then, between a student's understanding of the structures of language and their ability to comprehend the texts that they read indicates the necessity for teachers to provide students with impactful instruction on the structures of their language. It is key that this instruction is not purely about teaching grammar and rules for their own sake. In order for the instruction to be most powerful, it needs to be focused on understanding the rules so that students can most effectively understand texts that they will read. It is important to recognize that knowing the rules of a language not only leads to comprehension, but is also a key component of fluency. "Fluency is not a matter of speed; it is a matter of being able to utilize all the special knowledge a child has about a word—its letters, letter patterns, meanings, grammatical functions, roots and endings" (Wolf & Stoodley, 2017, pp. 130–131). It is for these reasons that educators should be concerned that explicit grammar instruction is typically lacking in many curricula.

LANGUAGE STRUCTURES IN A MONTESSORI CLASSROOM

Grammar in the 3–6 Classroom. In Montessori classrooms, children are introduced to grammar at an early age and at a time when they are fascinated by grammar and the way their language works. By the kindergarten year, students have already been introduced to the basic parts of speech and the "jobs" each of those have in their language. Dr. Montessori's grammar materials help to symbolize each of those parts of speech, which helps students to better grasp the abstract underpinnings of their language. Grammar, word study, and sentence analysis are important parts of the elementary Montessori curriculum. In a recent blog post, Montessori education advocate Lori Bourne makes this helpful analogy: "The study of grammar is to language what the study of anatomy is to science. By studying grammar, we become better writers and readers" (2022). It is with the focus of helping students become better readers and writers that from an early age and with the unique Montessori materials, children are highly engaged with the study of their language that middle and junior high school students often dread.

Grammar Symbols. As an example of the engaging nature of Montessori grammar materials, kindergartners are introduced to the parts of speech using a three-dimensional shape with a unique color and story behind it (Figure 8.1). They are first introduced to the *noun*. The symbol for the noun is a square-based black pyramid. The children are told this is like a pyramid, which was foundational to the early humans on Earth and is also foundational to sentences. It is black in color to represent carbon, the first mineral discovered by humans. It is likely nouns were also a first for humans to identify people, animals, plants, and locations within their local geography.

Once students have mastered the noun, the adjective, and the article, they are introduced to the *verb*. The symbol for the verb is a large red sphere. The teacher explains that the next type of words they are going to explore are

Figure 8.1. Grammar Symbols

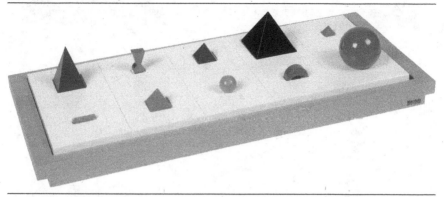

words that are all about movement, action, and doing. While sharing this with the students, the teacher then takes the large red sphere and gently lets it roll on the table, work rug, or activity mat. The teacher asks the students if the sphere is moving. And of course, the students indicate yes. Then the teacher gets out the large black pyramid representing the noun and asks the children, "Does the pyramid move?" The students respond in the negative. Next, by gently rolling the red sphere against the pyramid and making the pyramid move, the teacher says, "Look, the red sphere is moving the noun. Today, we are going to talk about words that have the job of telling us the noun's actions. They are action words, like push, pull, run, walk, and jump." The teacher can then tell the students that action words are called *verbs*.

Grammar in the 6–12 Classroom. In many Montessori schools, students arrive at first grade with an understanding of many parts of speech. The elementary teacher is likely to review the parts of speech and the relative roles in our language structures. A noun is referred to as a naming word, articles help us know if there is more than one object in a set, adjectives describe nouns, verbs are action words, prepositions tell us the position or relationship of one thing to something else, adverbs tell the *how* of performing an action, pronouns take the place of a noun or a noun phrase, conjunctions join words and phrases together, and interjections show emotion. Each has its own symbol, story, and purposes (Table 8.1). Each starts with a "Key Experience," which most students receive in the first grade. In Montessori, "Key Experiences" are a way of introducing a new concept to students in a way that sparks their imagination and, at the same time, sets the stage for further carefully scaffolded lessons.

After students have mastered the key experiences for any of the parts of speech, they can continue into more complexity of the given part of speech. In Montessori manuals, one could find about a dozen scaffolded lessons (or

Table 8.1. Grammar Symbol definitions

The Function of Words

noun	A noun names a person, place, thing, or an idea.
article	An article signifies the existence of a noun. The three articles are a, an, the.
adjective	An adjective describes a noun.
pronoun	A pronoun replaces a noun or another pronoun.
preposition	A preposition shows the connection between nouns, pronouns, and phrases to other words in a sentence.
verb	A verb conveys an action or an event.
adverb	An adverb describes a verb, an adjective, or an adverb.
conjunction	A conjunction connects words, phrases, and sentences.
interjection	An interjection is added to a verse to express an emotion.

Figure 8.2. Adjective Boxes

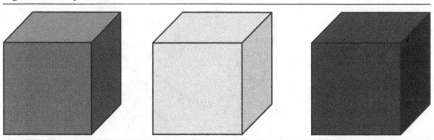

more) on each part of speech. For the purposes of this text, the authors will describe this progression highlighting a handful of the lessons contained in the series of scaffolded lessons using the adjective as an example.

Adjective Boxes. As previously mentioned, the first of the scaffolded lessons is the "Key Experience." The Adjective Key Experience has the teacher laying out three objects that are the same, except for their color (Figure 8.2). The teacher then asks one of the students to choose a box. When the student gives the teacher one of the boxes, the teacher in a dramatic and playful way says, "Thank you so much. That is a beautiful box, but it's not the one I wanted." The teacher again asks for the student to choose another box. Again, the teacher in a playful way says, "Thank you so much. That is a beautiful box, but it's not the one I wanted." The teacher then pauses, and dramatically modeling careful contemplation, and says, "Oh dear, you could not give me the box that I wanted because I did not give you enough information. I am so sorry. I hope you will forgive me!" The lesson continues with the teacher specifying by color which box should be chosen and explains to the students that those colors are describing the noun (box). Further, the teacher lets the learners know that words that describe nouns are called *adjectives*.

Noun Family. The "Noun Family" chart symbolizes the article (small light blue triangle), the adjective (medium dark blue triangle), and the noun (large black triangle). In this lesson, the objective is to understand the order of these parts of speeches in our sentences. The lesson begins with reviewing those parts of speeches and their relative roles in our language. As pictured, the chart depicts a mother (noun), daughter (adjective), and a younger and smaller daughter (article) happily joining hands and wearing the same "dresses" as the symbols that represent the parts of speeches they are depicting (Figure 8.3).

It is further explained that the very important noun is like the mother in the chart. Her oldest daughter would have come first and would have needed to hold her mother's hand. Then, the younger daughter comes along and she cannot walk yet without help from her big sister. So she holds her big sister's

Figure 8.3. Noun Family

article   adjective   noun

hand. They always show up in this order. Further, it is explained to the students that just as the daughters' existences depend on the mother, the article and adjective's existences depend on the noun. Students are then invited to make their own "Noun Family" charts and in future work identify wherever they see the "Noun Family."

Logical Adjective Game. Building on this lesson, students are taught to play the "Logical Adjective Game," where the objective is to match a set of cards with adjectives written on them to a set of cards with nouns written on them in ways that make sense. The noun cards (printed on black to be consistent with the black triangle noun symbol) might include words like flower, child, cat, car, snow, mouse, fish, sun, ball, bear, and bell. The adjective cards (printed on blue to be consistent with the blue triangle adjective symbol) might include words like heavy, pretty, cold, little, furry, soft, big, wet, hot, loud, and hungry (Figure 8.4). Students are then instructed to find a singular match for an adjective that "goes with" a noun and makes "logical sense." A correct match could be "hot sun" where an incorrect response could be "furry sun."

An extension of this activity is for the logical agreement to include more than one adjective for one specific noun. In this exercise, the teacher presents

Figure 8.4. Logical Adjective Game

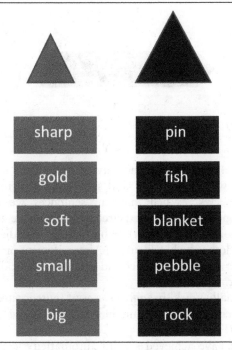

sharp	pin
gold	fish
soft	blanket
small	pebble
big	rock

one noun to the students, for instance, *sun*. Then the teacher presents multiple adjectives to the students, for instance, *hot, yellow, round, one, Earth's, beautiful*, and *large*. The teacher then might say, "All of these adjectives describe the sun," and then turn to the students and curiously ask them, "What order should these adjectives be in?" A discussion then ensues as the teacher and the students discuss their thoughts about the proper order of the adjectives. The discussion may lead to the proper order just from the way the words sound. The teacher can then introduce the proper order of adjectives: number, opinion, size, age, shape, and color. Accordingly, the discussion leads to "one, beautiful, large, round, yellow sun."

Sentence Analysis. Another way the Montessori curriculum addresses language structures is through lessons in sentence analysis. The introduction is purposely simple and includes only unmarked red (for the verb) and black (for the noun) circles and black arrows (Figure 8.5).

The teacher places the circles and arrows on a demonstration surface and asks a child one thing they see happening in the classroom. A student may respond, "Jackie is writing." The teacher then responds, "Oh, so in the sentence 'Jackie is writing,' **the action is** *writing*," and shows the students

Figure 8.5. Sentence Analysis Symbols

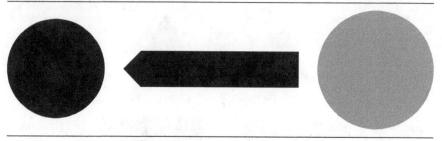

the large red circle. Then the teacher says, "And in the sentence 'Jackie is writing,' Jackie is **who is writing**," and shows the students the large black circle. The teacher says, "When analyzing sentences, we always start with the action," while pointing to the red circle, "and then we go to" (as they lay down the arrow pointing to the left) "who or what it is that is doing the action" (as they lay down the black circle). After sufficient practice, the teacher introduces the idea of a direct object and eventually introduces the students to the terms *predicate* and *subject*.

Students gradually work through a series of sentence analysis (using a set of labeled red circles, black circles, and black arrows, as well as a corresponding chart) lessons (Figure 8.6).

Once children have achieved a solid automaticity with these activities, the teacher can begin adding adverbial modifiers that support the analysis of phrases in sentences pertaining to agency, instrument, accomplishment, source, place, cause, purpose, and manner.

EXEMPLAR STRUCTURED LITERACY ACTIVITIES: LANGUAGE STRUCTURES

While explicit grammar instruction is not typically fully included in the current educational landscape, there are common curricula that address language structure in a systematic study of sentence structure. For example, the Language Circle teaches its form of sentence diagramming in Project Read (Language Circle Enterprises). Project Read is a Structured Literacy Intervention that provides explicit and systematic phonics instruction, including syllable types and division patterns. This intervention acknowledges that reading is not exclusively phonics instruction and includes various elements of other strands from Scarborough's Reading Rope.

Students are taught to code sentences by locating and marking nouns and verbs. Sentence frames and paragraph frames are utilized to support the use of capitals, ending punctuation, and paragraphs. Writing curricula such as

Figure 8.6. Sentence Analysis Symbols Applied

One subject, one predicate:

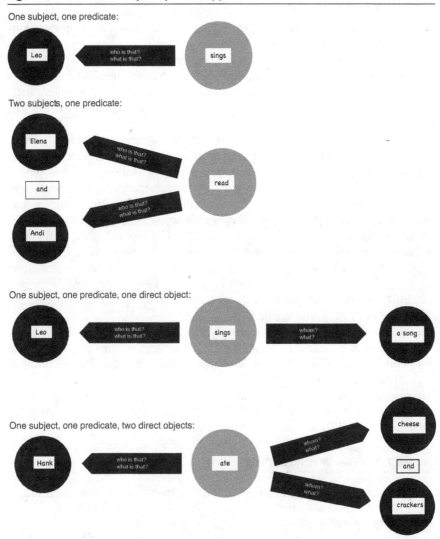

Two subjects, one predicate:

One subject, one predicate, one direct object:

One subject, one predicate, two direct objects:

Step Up to Writing have a similar component. Students' attention is drawn to the structures of word arrangement. Sentence structure is referred to as "syntax."

Additionally, various diagnostic and progress-monitoring assessments include syntax as a piece of reading comprehension. In the DIBELS Maze assessment, students select the correct word from three options that would appropriately fill in the blank of a sentence. One of the three choices is often a word that is syntactically incorrect. The purpose behind this option is to determine whether students consider the language structure in their responses.

For students with a wide exposure to language, using conventional language structure may feel "natural." Some students say they can just "feel" how a sentence should sound. Even so, explicit instruction in language structures and grammar assists all students with text comprehension and written expression. Importantly, multilanguage learners may need support in language structures. Common grammatical errors may reflect the language structures of the first language.

This includes children who speak African American English (AAE). Dr. Julie Washington is an expert in the role dialect plays in the identification of reading disabilities in African American children and on the development of early language skills and reading for children, especially those negatively impacted by the effects of poverty. As educators, we all need to recognize that speaking another language or dialect is only an obstacle when the learning needs are not attended to. Teachers can provide support to multilanguage- and multidialect-speaking students by assuring sufficient learning opportunities, utilizing instructional practices and resources that will be effective given the background students bring to their learning experiences, and, very importantly, "eliminating the unwarranted stigma associated with using AAE" (Washington & Seidenberg, 2021).

Syntax refers to the rules of how words are organized and arranged to create logical and meaningful sentences. The research comprising the Science of Reading reveals that syntax is developed in the early years. The Common Core State Standards include grammar instruction in the language strand. For example, L.K.1e states that kindergarten students will use the most frequently occurring prepositions. Figure 8.7 shows two ways instruction in prepositions can be incorporated into the classroom.

Figure 8.7. Activities With Prepositions

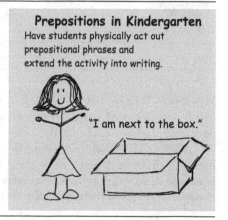

L.K.4b states that, in kindergarten, students will use the most frequently occurring inflections and affixes. Inflections and affixes often show word tense or plurality. Word-building activities allow students to manipulate the way a word is used in a sentence—for example, changing it from a noun to an adjective. Affixes hold meaning that can designate the grammatical use of the word. Words can be changed by applying inflections and affixes.

The structure of a sentence may give students difficulty because of its complex arrangement. Most frequently this would include sentences that begin with a prepositional phrase or contain a relative clause. A sentence such as "Prior to going to bed, I did the dishes" contains information that is out of sequential time order. Even though the sentence talks about going to bed first, the dishes were the first activity being completed.

One of the best ways to instruct in these complex text structures is to take sentences from classroom text and make sure students are aware of how the sentence is set up and what it actually is telling them. In the understanding of language structure, it is most important to draw attention to the way a sentence is created and how the structures influence the meaning of that sentence. Guided questioning regarding structure can unobtrusively be added into any lesson.

Both the comprehension of text and the ability to express oneself in writing are contingent on being able to understand and create complex sentence structure. The ability to understand language structure contributes to the development of a strong reader.

CHAPTER 9

Verbal Reasoning

SCIENCE OF READING—VERBAL REASONING

As students master word recognition skills, they must also simultaneously engage in activities that support comprehension development. The National Reading Panel (NICHD, 2000) pointed to longstanding evidence that reading comprehension requires both vocabulary knowledge and reasoning (p. 228, 4–3). Scarborough (2001) also stressed the need for coordination between the cognitive–linguistic strands of the Reading Rope, which she labeled Word Recognition and Language Comprehension, respectively. Notably, students "with weaker verbal abilities and literacy knowledge are much more likely than their classmates to experience difficulties in learning to read" (p. 100). From the earliest stages of a student's academic career, instruction focused on word recognition skills combined with comprehension strategies supports the development of a competent reader.

Scarborough's verbal reasoning strand includes *inference* and *metaphor* as indicators of this skill that can be defined as the "ability to infer or draw a conclusion from known or assumed facts" (Marcotte et al., 2017, p. 2218). In the classroom, your 3rd-grade student correctly pronounces and decodes all the letter strings in a passage, but they may not be successful at comprehending what they've read if:

- They do not know the word in their spoken language.
- They are not able to makes sense of the syntactic and semantic connections between the words.
- They lack the "critical background knowledge or inferential skills to interpret the text appropriately." (Scarborough, 2001, p. 98)

Without these skills, students often lack the ability to understand information not explicitly stated in the text (inferences), abstract concepts, or even the purpose of the information shared in the text.

Comprehension. Early readers focus most of their efforts on sounding out and reading each phonetic word so as to understand what's being shared in a sentence. But soon after, readers begin to encounter text that implies meaning rather than stating it explicitly.

Looking at data prior to the impact of the COVID-19 pandemic on education and students learning, the 2019 National Assessment of Educational Progress (NAEP) reported that over a third of 4th-grade students in the United States were reading below NAEP Basic. This designation means that 4th-grade students were unable to locate relevant information in a text, make simple inferences, or use their understanding of the text to identify details that supported a given interpretation or conclusion. When reading informational texts, they were unable to identify the main idea or gather information from the text to provide supporting evidence. Similarly, when reading poetry or nonfiction, they were unable to make simple inferences about characters, events, plot, or setting (U.S. Department of Education, 2019).

Since so much of what students will learn during their academic careers comes through successfully reading and comprehending text, reading comprehension is a critical skill for academic success.

Inferencing. As a predictor of reading comprehension, inferencing is the "process by which a reader integrates information from the text with background knowledge in order to fill in details and links not explicitly stated in a text" (Smith et al., 2021, p. 216). You may have heard inferencing compared to "reading between the lines."

For example, while listening to a story read aloud, students are told the character in the story is preparing for an event. There are balloons, wrapped gifts, and a cake from the bakery with 10 candles ready to be lit. From the description, students can infer there will be a birthday celebration, without those actual words being written in the text. Inferencing requires the reader to make logical steps in deducing a conclusion by filling in details not stated in the text (Segers & Verhoeven, 2016).

A reader must integrate multiple skills to comprehend inferred text, such as background or world knowledge of the topic, a depth of vocabulary, and the ability to contextualize these skills based on the words, phrases, and actions from the text (Cain, 2021).

VERBAL REASONING IN A MONTESSORI CLASSROOM

As described in the previous section, students first learn to decode letter strings on the page—learning to read—with text that is literal and easily understood. But as students progress through the elementary grades and beyond, reading becomes the vehicle for learning. "Reading material in all subject areas conveys information and ideas that students are expected to learn and understand. When students are unable to understand these texts, they miss crucial opportunities to learn grade-level content" (Vaughn et al., 2022, p. 20).

One strength of the Montessori curriculum is the range and depth of content that builds background knowledge and vocabulary development—key components of reading with comprehension. In Chapter 7 and Chapter 8, we reviewed Montessori materials such as Nomenclature Three-Part Cards, labeled picture cards with matching objects, definition cards, and booklets that build background knowledge and vocabulary related to zoology, geography, botany, and geometry, and the categorization of objects that can be found within the child's home, school, and community environment.

The Montessori *Who Am I?* stories provide students with an opportunity to practice both reading and reasoning skills. The student, working on their own or with another student, reads through the description card that provides 3–5 short sentences describing, but not naming, a particular object or animal. For example, the card might read: "I am a nocturnal mammal that feeds on insects and fruit. Unlike most mammals, I can fly. And when I fly at night, I use a special way to 'see' in the dark called echolocation." After reading the definition card, the student would then match it to the correct image and label (bat). A control card, a separate card that contains all the correct information, is available for students to self-assess their understanding.

Careful review of the literature shows that research related to Scarborough's verbal reasoning strand and comprehension strategies from the wider education community will benefit the Montessori Language curriculum. The next section offers additional Science of Reading verbal reasoning activities, including two recommendations from the Institute of Education Sciences (IES) report (Vaughn et al., 2022), *Providing Reading Interventions for Students in Grades 4–9*.

EXEMPLAR STRUCTURED LITERACY ACTIVITIES: VERBAL REASONING

Inferring falls within the analyzing level of Bloom's Taxonomy. As teachers address Bloom's higher levels of questioning and comprehension, they have the opportunity to directly instruct the skill of inferencing. In the pre-reading stages, this is frequently done by analyzing illustrations to describe what is happening in a scene. Jan Brett's picture books, such as *The Mitten* (2009), *The Snowy Nap* (2018), and *The Hat* (1997), are ideal for this type of activity. Hiding in the illustrations, there is extra information about the story that is not found in the text. Teachers tell students to see if they can find any clues about what else is happening in the story; students become detectives.

When students compare before-and-after pictures with the goal of determining what happened and how/why, they infer what has happened. Selected sentence starters can help students make the connection between what they read/see and what they know. Sentence frames may include: "It seems like . . . ," "I would guess . . . ," "This could mean/show . . . ," and "I would predict/infer. . . ."

Graphic Organizers. Graphic organizers can structure this comprehension detective work. Students record what they read or see in the text, what they know about that "thing" (connections they have to the reading/picture that activate prior knowledge), and finally record what inferences they can draw. An example might be a picture of a city with a tornado in the background (Table 9.1).

Visual Thinking Strategies. Once a week, *The New York Times* publishes an online inferencing photograph in their "What's Going on in this Picture?" posting. These photos or other photos gleaned from books or the Internet can open a conversation that connects students' reasoning by linking their current knowledge base to the information provided to them. Older students can even join in an online discussion building off of each other as they speculate about the context and meaning behind the given image. (Visit https://www.nytimes.com/column/learning-whats-going-on-in-this-picture.)

Similarly, wordless books are wonderful for inferencing skills. The Caldecott Honor Book *Journey*, by Aaron Becker, along with its two sequels, *Quest* and *Return*, provide a plethora of intricate and engaging illustrations around which student discussion will yield a high level of inferences. Similarly, Chris Van Allsburg offers enigmatic illustrations in his portfolio *The Mysteries of Harris Burdick* and storylines that necessitate inference such as *The Sweetest Fig*.

It is a skill in and of itself to differentiate the subtleties of various word choices (Common Core Standard L.K.5d). Younger students can distinguish shades of meaning among verbs describing the same general action by acting out their meanings. The Common Core gives one example to show how this standard might look in kindergarten instruction. Given the verbs *walk*, *march*, *strut*, and *prance*, students analyze how these actions differ from one another in subtle ways and demonstrate that difference by acting them out. Authors choose verbs with variations in meaning to portray specific feelings and actions. Students can find those words and describe what the author means. This activity simultaneously builds vocabulary. A teacher can provide a starting verb, for example, "write," and students can verbalize words that mean the same thing . . . *scribble*, *mark*, *note*. Such subtleties are important within the Four-Part Processor. When students identify a word and use

Table 9.1. Graphic Organizer to Support Inferencing

What I see/read	There is a town with buildings. There is a tornado in the distance. People are pointing at the tornado. They are not smiling.
What I know	Tornadoes move fast. Tornadoes can knock down buildings.
Inference	The tornado could move to the town and knock down the buildings. The people are pointing and not smiling because they are afraid the tornado will come to their town.

context to determine meaning, the slight shades of meaning influence how the sentence is interpreted.

Verbal reasoning also includes being able to select the contextually appropriate meaning for words (using the context processor in the Four-Part Processor model). *Amelia Bedelia* books are a classic way of showing how important context clues can be in determining the meaning of a word. Students synthesize the information in multiple sentences, making connections within the given text and connections to their prior knowledge in order to determine what meaning a word takes.

Take the following example:

> Molly and Dave were excited for their trip. Molly wanted to see the monkeys and Dave wanted to see the lions. They packed lunch and put on their sneakers. Molly and Dave were ready to walk around and visit the wild animals all day.
> Where were Molly and Dave going?

Clues from the paragraph connect with the students' knowledge of zoos and enable the leap to understand that Molly and Dave will be going to the zoo.

Recommendations From the Institute of Education Sciences (IES). A 2022 report from IES, the research arm of the U.S. Department of Education, offers additional evidence-based practices that can support all elementary and middle school educators to meet the needs of their students who are not yet proficient readers. The report, *Providing Reading Interventions for Students in Grade 4–9* (Vaughn et al., 2022), made four recommendations:

- Recommendation 1: Build students' decoding skills so they can read complex multisyllabic words.
- Recommendation 2: Provide purposeful fluency-building activities to help students read effortlessly.
- Recommendation 3: Routinely use a set of comprehension-building practices to help students make sense of the text.
- Recommendation 4: Provide students with opportunities to practice making sense of stretch text (i.e., challenging text) that will expose them to complex ideas and information.

These recommendations span the scope of Scarborough's Reading Rope, once again emphasizing that the Science of Reading is not limited to phonics. While phonics and automaticity of decoding (fluency) are an important part of how one can meet the needs of struggling readers, direct instruction and support in the language comprehension skill strand of the Reading Rope is given as much attention.

Thus, for the purposes of this chapter, the focus will be on Recommendations 3 and 4.

Recommendation 3: Routinely use a set of comprehension-building practices to help students make sense of the text. The goal of the recommendation is to provide educators with instructional routines to help their students "learn and practice routines and develop reading habits that enable students to understand what they are reading" (Vaughn et al., 2022, p. 20). This recommendation focuses on four strategies. The first looks at improving vocabulary and background knowledge (Part A), while the remaining three strategies develop comprehension-building practices (Parts B, C, and D).

Recommendation 3, Part A. Build students' world and word knowledge so they can make sense of the text. This part of the recommendation focuses on building background knowledge related to topics students read, along with specific vocabulary associated with the text. "Some students may have difficulty comprehending text not because they struggle to read, but because they have limited knowledge of the topic of the text or do not know the meanings of words" (Vaughn, 2022, p. 22). The panel makes three recommendations to educators:

IES recommends that teachers "Develop world knowledge that is relevant for sense making" (Vaughn, 2022, p. 22). This instruction can include a brief introduction on the topic before reading, perhaps asking students to read an easier passage before offering a higher-level text. A teacher could provide a short video clip, podcast, or images to supplement a brief introductory lecture. This targeted piece of instruction should be succinct and convey information necessary to access the text. However, instruction should be pointed and brief, for this is not the lesson or reading itself, but the pre-reading instruction that prepares the student and ensures that all students have the information needed to access the meaning of the text. For example, if the text to be studied is set on the beach, it is worthwhile to confirm that all students have a general knowledge of what the "beach" is. It is not necessary to spend 30 minutes having each student describe a personal experience at the beach. The development of world knowledge is ultimately aimed at establishing a common starting place as the student enters the text. Certainly, this is supporting equity within the classroom; all students have the knowledge they need to unlock the author's textual meaning.

Second, IES recommends one "teach the meaning of a few words that are essential for understanding the passage" (Vaughn, 2022, p. 24). Identify words from the text that may be difficult for students but that are critical to know if they are to understand the text. Before reading, provide a simple definition and example as it relates to the text for one or two essential words. If additional words are defined during reading, it should be done very quickly to "ensure that the unfamiliar word does not disrupt comprehension" (p. 24).

One should also "teach students how to derive meanings of unknown words using context" (Vaughn, 2022, p. 26). Educators can demonstrate this using a three-step strategy to use surrounding text to gather information. First, have the student identify the word they don't understand in the text. Next, ask the student to reread the sentence to see if there are other words that can provide clues. And last, if that sentence does not contain enough information, ask the student to read the sentence before and after the unknown word to identify other meaningful clues. If there is still not enough information, the student can always look up the word for a more formal definition.

Using the morphology of the unknown word is an important skill students can use that will enable them to expand their vocabulary independently. IES states that teachers should "Teach students prefixes and suffixes to help students derive meanings of words" (Vaughn, 2022, p. 29). This knowledge will help students read and understand multisyllabic words. Additionally, they recommend that teachers "Teach the meaning of Latin and Greek roots" (p. 34). Because so many English words derive from other languages, it benefits students if there is explicit instruction in root words and their meanings. Online tools may be found that allow students to manipulate meaningful word parts (morphemes) to change a word's meaning.

The positive correlation between vocabulary and comprehension is shown time and again in reading research (Coyne & Loftus-Rattan, 2022). Not only must one provide the direct instruction of vocabulary, one must provide students with the tools (e.g., understanding morphological word units) to teach themselves new words.

Recommendation 3, Part B. Consistently provide students with opportunities to ask and answer questions to better understand the text they read. The goal of this recommendation is to help students learn to "draw text-based interpretations or inferences about what the author implied" (Vaughn et al., 2022, p. 37).

Educators can consider explicitly teaching students how to find and justify answers to different types of questions from within the text. Three question types are suggested: (a) the Right There question, where information is located explicitly in the text; (b) the Think and Share question, where information is located in different parts of the text; and (c) the Author and Me question, which asks students to connect information they've learned previously with information found in the text (Vaughn et al., 2022, p. 37).

Teachers must provide ample opportunities for students to collaboratively answer questions. Ask students to work together to identify specific text that will serve as justification for their responses (Vaughn et al., 2022, p. 41).

Recommendation 3, Part C. Teach students a routine for determining the gist of a short section of text. Sometimes called the "Get the Gist Strategy," producing a gist statement prompts students to "synthesize the most important information in a short one- or two-paragraph section of the text. Some refer to it as the main idea" (Vaughn et al., 2022, p. 47).

In this recommendation, IES suggests teachers should "model how to use a routine to generate gist statements" (Vaughn et al., 2022, p. 47) and teach students how to use text structures to generate them. "Teachers can model and create prompts to guide students to identify the most important information in the text" (p. 51).

Extensive work to develop teaching materials that support "get the gist" instruction have been created through the Content-Area Literacy Instruction (CALI) project (https://projectcali.uconn.edu). Models and guiding prompts/scripts can be found as part of this grant work. The IRIS Center (https://iris.peabody.vanderbilt.edu) has created a module devoted to Get the Gist and lays out four steps students go through to understand the main idea being presented and to restate that main idea in 10 or fewer words.

Recommendation 3, Part D. Teach students to monitor their comprehension as they read. Students need self-awareness about their own comprehension of text.

Educators can help students determine when they do not understand text. Teachers may have students read sentences, including those that are nonsensical, to determine if they can understand the text. For example, when presenting a sentence such as "The quiffles gumped along the road and smeepily shreved each other," ask, "What gumped along the road?" (Students respond, "The quiffles.") "What did the quiffles do with each other?" (Students respond, "They shreved.") "How did the quiffles shreve each other?" (Students respond, "Smeepily.") Even though this sentence is nonsense, the students' knowledge of text structure will help them answer these questions. Teachers can then ask students to describe a quiffle. As quiffles don't exist, students will be unable to do this. The teacher can make the point that students recognize they do not understand this text even though they could answer some questions about it. Students need to be aware of the depth of understanding a text as they read.

And one can teach students to ask themselves questions as they read to check their understanding and figure out what the text is about.

Recommendation 4: Provide students with opportunities to practice making sense of stretch text (i.e., challenging text) that will expose them to complex ideas and information. Teachers can prepare for the lesson by carefully selecting appropriate stretch texts, choosing points to stop for discussion and clarification, and identifying words to teach.

This is a prime opportunity to select texts representative of the students' cultural and linguistic backgrounds. Consider the recommendation to look at the major themes being discussed in a text as well as the purpose the text will have in instruction (e.g., is the student reading the entire book independently? Is the student closely reading only a single paragraph or chapter?), as discussed in the Common Core State Standards (2010).

Choose texts that are close to topics currently being studied. Stretch texts can be found on sites like http://newsela.com and http://readwords.com. Prepare two or three essential words that are critical to understanding the text and review them prior to reading. Also, identify any multisyllabic words that will reinforce students' recent reading skills.

As students demonstrate confidence reading stretch texts in groups, provide electronic supports for use when reading independently. For example, iPads and computers are fitted with electronic dictionaries to support word learning and pronunciation of words. Some software may provide word origins to help students determine an unknown word's meaning, whereas others may read portions of text aloud as the student follows along in their text.

Verbal reasoning skills target the ability to make sense of the text, truly the purpose behind all reading.

CHAPTER 10

Literacy Knowledge

There are many aspects of literacy that, by adulthood, are assimilated unconsciously. The understanding of how print is used in day-to-day life becomes a part of one's identity.

SCIENCE OF READING—LITERACY KNOWLEDGE

Scarborough's Reading Rope labels readers' understanding of print concepts and genres as components of the literacy knowledge strand. As defined by *Preventing Reading Difficulties in Young Children* (1998), concepts of print are "a set of understandings about the conventions of literacy, e.g., directionality, intentionality, stability, use of blank spaces and letters, and multiple genres and uses" (p. 317). These print concept skills build a more global understanding of how print can be used, rather than building knowledge of specific letters.

Interacting with Adults and Peers in Authentic Literacy Situations. For younger children, building literacy knowledge can be facilitated by providing learning environments that encourage the practice of interacting with adults and peers in reading and writing situations in early childhood classrooms and in daily life. This could include exploring printed words, pretending to read a book, and experimenting with using different types of written language. These interactions reveal a child's growing understanding of the purposes of the written word and serve as a gateway into literacy (Neuman & Roskos, 1997).

Environmental Print Is Not a First Stage of Reading. Before children begin formal schooling, they are surrounded by print in their environment, such as newspapers and magazines, children's books, and logos of favorite cereals or children's television shows—all of which serve to expose young children to print. But exposure is not enough; students need to be taught print concepts. An early study of 3–5-year-old children's understanding of print in the ecology of their lived environments demonstrated that even the most skilled "readers" of logos (examples included the word "McDonald's," with the M substituted with the golden arches logo; the word "STOP" written on a street sign; and the words "Crayola Crayons" written on a box of crayons) were no longer successful readers when the color, logo shape, font, and other context cues were removed (Masonheimer et al., 1984). Children do not become successful readers through repeated exposures to environmental print. Rather, children are successful readers when they have a working understanding of the alphabetic principle, or letter-sound correspondence, phonemic awareness, and other conventions of literacy such as directionality of print. Interestingly, a later study conducted by Reutzel and colleagues (2003) proposed that even children who have well-established word-reading strategies may not transfer phonics skills when reading environmental print. Instead, reading environmental print may rely on a "largely dominant visual orientation with attention to graphic detail but not using letter-sound knowledge" (p. 157). As with any print material made available in classrooms, it is not enough for it to be displayed for students. Rather, there needs to be explicit word study and decoding instruction to help students become proficient readers of all available print.

LITERACY KNOWLEDGE IN A MONTESSORI CLASSROOM

So, what print concept components do Montessori educators focus on in the classroom? Enz and Morrow (2009, p. 76) described pre- and early-reading skills that require explicit instruction that teachers can use to document learning in a Montessori classroom, including graphic awareness; writing and connections to conventions of print; and emergent reading, concepts of books, and connections to concepts of print; as well as an understanding of the alphabetic principle.

Graphic Awareness. Graphic awareness is an understanding that print carries meaning. Young children demonstrate graphic awareness when they use scribbles and parts of letters to "write" their name or grocery lists as part of their play. Classrooms must offer both engaging materials and authentic opportunities for young writers to capture their thinking on paper. This can include different sizes and colors of paper available in multiple locations around the classroom, along with small clipboards and pencils readily available for children to note observations. One authentic writing opportunity is the availability of "Parts of . . ." books as extensions of the many nomenclature cards that build students' background knowledge and vocabulary (see Chapter 7). And many Montessori and conventional schools use Handwriting Without Tears (Olsen et al., 2003), a program to support children's writing skills.

Writing and Its Connection to Conventions of Print. Conventions of print include explicitly demonstrating for students that when writing in English, words move from left to write and top to bottom on a page, that each new sentence begins with a capital letter, and that spaces are placed between words to make our written ideas understandable to others.

In a Montessori classroom, the large Movable Alphabet introduces students to encoding practices by sounding out individual phonemes of three- and four-letter phonetic words (bat, cup, dog) and placing small wooden letters on a mat to *make* a word (see Chapter 4, "Decoding"). The prefabricated letters support the youngest pre-readers to build decoding and writing skills, while they simultaneously continue to build fine motor development to successfully write with a pencil. As students become more proficient, they extend their work of making words with the Movable Alphabet to then writing their words on paper. When students are ready to compose more complete thoughts in the form of paragraphs or short stories, they will then move on to use the Small Movable Alphabet (Figure 10.1).

Similar in design, the letters in the Small Movable Alphabet are premade and vowels and consonants are distinguished by color (blue and red, respectively). However, the sensorial feature of each letter shape is no longer needed by the student, and each letter is placed on an individual plastic tile with the lowercase printed on one side of the tile and the uppercase letter printed on the back.

Authentic writing opportunities with the Small Movable Alphabet can include any topic of interest to the child, from writing an invitation to another child to join them at the park that afternoon, to describing the animals and events they saw at a recent visit to the zoo, to offering a reflection of a chapter book completed during morning work time. The teacher is available to support

Figure 10.1. Using the Small Movable Alphabet to Support Writing Conventions

Image courtesy of Central Montessori Academy.

the student, as needed. When the student is ready, they will review their work with the teacher, who then notes competence in writing conventions and provides individualized instruction related to punctuation, word spacing, and capitalization. These writing opportunities also serve as formative assessments of students' grammar, understanding of contractions, and overall spelling development, which in turn will inform future student-centered instruction.

Emergent Reading and Concepts about Books. Emergent reading, concepts about books, and the connection to concepts of print begin with the youngest students' understanding and care for all classroom books. The students are able to identify the cover of the book. There's predictability in locating the author's name and the title of the book. And they understand where to begin reading on a page and the progression of reading words across a page (left to right/top to bottom). In Montessori Grace & Courtesy lessons, students learn the proper way to hold a book, to turn its pages, and to return it properly to the shelf so that it's ready for the next person to use.

In a Montessori classroom, new topics are often introduced through individual and small-group lessons and are reinforced in occasional whole-group settings. For example, the teacher may have offered a Care of Books lesson to a small group of children earlier in the morning. When the classroom meets as a whole group prior to the end of the day to read a story aloud, the teacher may reinforce the morning small-group lesson by demonstrating the proper handling of the book they have selected to read. These whole-group book reading opportunities offer authentic moments to highlight other book concepts, such as noting the book's title, noting the author and illustrator, and sharing that the author has used bold-faced or oversized fonts to indicate that a character is shouting excitedly.

Alphabetic Principle. The youngest students in the Montessori 3–6 classroom are introduced to the alphabetic principle when they begin to work with Sandpaper Letters (see Chapter 4, "Decoding"). As they trace the letter shape and repeat the letter sounds, children as young as 3 years old learn that letters have a relationship with sounds/phonemes. In time, with the use of the Movable Alphabet, Classification Cards, and other Montessori Language materials, students also learn that letters are used in particular combinations to create words, and these individual words develop sentences.

The next section provides additional literacy knowledge activities that align to Montessori educational practices to support classroom teaching.

EXEMPLAR STRUCTURED LITERACY ACTIVITIES: LITERACY KNOWLEDGE

Modeling and Explicit Instruction. In the Structured Literacy classroom, early print concepts are taught through modeling. Teachers narrate how one

Figure 10.2. Explicitly Charting Concepts of Print

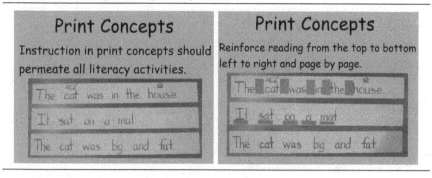

Figure 10.3. Multisensory Sandpaper Letters for Learning Letter Shapes

approaches text by talking through how they pick up a book, turn pages, and track top to bottom and left to right. Formal concepts of print are addressed in Common Core Standard RF.K.1a-c: (a) follow words from left to right, top to bottom, and page by page, (b) recognize spoken words are represented in written language by specific sequences of letters, and (c) understand that words are separated by spaces in print.

Along with modeling and exposure to print skills, students may explicitly identify conventions of print. They may place sticky notes between words in written text to represent the spaces. They may mark up shared text on chart paper by underlining or highlighting words to show how letters are grouped together into words (Figure 10.2).

Multisensory Activities. Core curriculum in the Structured Literacy classroom explores forming letters, matching letters to their sounds, and manipulating letters. Multisensory practices of letter writing include air writing; drawing letters in sand, salt, and/or shaving cream; and tracing raised letters on letter cards (often sandpaper or dried glue) (Figure 10.3). Air writing (also

Figure 10.4. Salt Trays to Practice Letter Formations

referred to as "sky writing") has students hold one arm out straight in front of them with their first two fingers extended as if they were going to push a button. They draw the letter in the air while saying its name and sound. Using the whole arm to do this makes air writing a gross motor skill and allows the teacher to see if students are forming the letters correctly.

Paper plates filled with a thin layer of salt or sand make an inexpensive and individual workstation for students to practice letter formation (Figure 10.4).

English as an alphabetic language demands knowledge of the letter-sound correspondences. In truth, the sound of the letter or letter combinations is much more important than the name of that letter. Fundations, Project Read, and Really Great Reading, as well as many other curricula, all include word work with an emphasis on letter-sound correspondence.

As students develop proficiency with letters, word creation and the manipulation of letters within words follow quickly. Students practice with letter tiles or magnetic letters. Consider using half-size cookie sheets with these manipulatives for individual workstations.

All students progress through stages of word learning. It is important to recognize where a student is currently functioning and to look for opportunities to move the student forward. Both writing samples and spelling inventories (such as the Words Their Way Spelling Inventory) will help the teacher identify the current level of functioning. A spelling inventory looks like a traditional spelling test that progresses in difficulty. It is used as a diagnostic assessment and allows the teacher to determine phonics skills that students have mastered to the level of being able to use the skills in their writing (encoding). Having determined areas of mastery and need, a teacher can instruct what would be most helpful to specific learners.

Literary Devices and Genre Conventions. Literacy knowledge extends into a child's understanding of literary devices and genre conventions. For example, through exposure to read-alouds, a young child may recognize that a story has a character, a setting, a problem, and an ending. Simple activities to recall story structure such as the Somebody, Wanted, But, So, Then, Finally Strategy will support this understanding. As described in the book *When Kids Can't Read* (Beers, 2003), after reading a fiction story, prompt students to fill in the frame in a similar manner to Figure 10.5.

Students should be taught that other books are not stories. Nonfiction books give information and facts on something they want to know more about. Using concept mapping, top-down webs, and data collection tables allows students to see the organization of the facts that are provided. The Read-Around the Text Strategy, developed by Amy Goodman (2005) for use with older elementary and middle school students, calls attention to the structure of nonfiction texts as a pre-reading activity. Students note text features and internalize why the author added those features and what they tell us before reading the full text. Using this strategy, students take a nonfiction text and go through six steps in order to familiarize themselves with the format of the article, to activate prior knowledge, and to set a purpose for reading. The six steps include looking at the illustrations, graphs, charts, maps, and subtitles; reading headings, titles, and first/last sentences of paragraphs; and formulating questions to consider during the actual reading of the text.

Advanced genre studies, supported by core instruction, begin with a general knowledge gained through experience and grow to in-depth genre studies such as units on fairy tales or fables. A rich literacy environment enables

Figure 10.5. The Somebody, Wanted, But, So, Then, Finally Strategy

(Somebody)	Goldilocks
wanted	to see what was in the house,
but	no one was home.
So,	she ate the porridge and sat in the chairs.
Then,	she fell asleep in the smallest bed.
Finally,	the three bears came home and Goldilocks ran away.

children to be exposed to literacy knowledge that will ultimately support their reading comprehension. Tracking the genre of texts the student reads or that are read in the classroom may facilitate a growing understanding of genres. By 3rd grade, students should be able to differentiate between genres such as fairy tales, fables, and myths. This ability requires a deep knowledge of genre and the nuances that differentiate types of reading and writing.

This last skill of the Language Structures strand is not only important for students' reading ability but is also closely tied to the students' ability to generate text themselves. Reading and writing serve to communicate one's thoughts and ideas to others. It is the set of English conventions, print concepts, and text structures that situates ideas, information, and stories in a context that can be understood.

PART II CONCLUSION

To summarize the Language Comprehension portion of this book, the authors have discussed and provided examples of instructional practices from both Montessori education and the Science of Reading in the areas of background knowledge, vocabulary, language structures, verbal reasoning, and literacy knowledge. As Scarborough's Reading Rope illustrates, these Language Comprehension skills are entwined with one another. The resulting Language Comprehension strands are then entwined with the Word Recognition strands. Importantly, it should be noted that the strands are interdependent of one another, just as the major strands of Word Recognition and Language Comprehension can be considered mutually dependent. Therefore, if just one strand is weak, the entire Language Comprehension strand is undermined. Similarly, if either one of the two major strands (Word Recognition and Language Comprehension) is frail, the result is an inability to read at even a rudimentary level. The implications of this mutual dependence are paramount for consideration by policymakers and educational leaders. While well intended, they often and incorrectly overreduce, or eliminate, social studies and science instruction in the early grades so that instructional hours on Word Recognition skills can be increased. Advocacy from every person well versed in the implications of the mutually dependent relationship between Word Recognition and Language Comprehension will be necessary to ensure that every child receives instruction in Language Comprehension skills.

In the following closing chapter, the authors hope that the discussion serves as a call for shared and united work in ensuring every child has access to instruction rooted in the Science of Reading. This collaborative effort will require all of us to critically reflect on our own practices, actively break down silos, and openly engage with one another.

CHAPTER 11

Conclusion

SCIENTIFIC THINKING, DISCOURSE, AND ADVOCACY
TO IMPROVE THE LIVES OF CHILDREN

As we introduced ourselves and this book, we indicated that it was our de-sire to celebrate and strengthen the amazing work that happens in learning environments every day. Our intention was to share our findings and connec-tions as we considered and explored the instructional approaches based in the Science of Reading and the Montessori Method. Additionally, we hoped that we will be able set the stage for supporting an important relationship between educators who utilize research-based practices in both more conven-tional and Montessori classrooms.

As we described the similarities that have grown out of our research, work, and discussions regarding the parallels between Montessori education and the Science of Reading, we hoped to provide food for thought for our read-ers (teachers, administrators, policymakers, or researchers) as well as to set the stage for considering even more connections between the two approaches that use a scientific approach as a basis for considering teaching and learning. To further illustrate these points, we've developed the Montessori Materials and Science of Reading Matrix[2] (to access the PDF, please see the link and QR code provided below).

We recognize that context matters and that science can greatly establish and inform parameters for best practices in our field. However, as educators, we do need the freedom to make decisions in each of our contexts within the parameters that the body of research provides us. Cognitive psychologist Daniel Willingham compares this to the work of an architect who uses "the principles of physics and designing an office building, but will also be guided by aesthetic principles and by her budget" (2009, p. 278). Similarly, as educa-tors we would be wise to work within the parameters that are afforded to us by the overwhelming evidence that points to the need for instructional prac-tices that feature clarity, explicit systematic instruction, timely feedback, and guided and independent practice. However, within

---

2. To access the **Montessori Materials and Science of Reading Matrix**, please use the following link https://qrco.de/bdMRCP or scan this QR code.

those parameters, we each must carefully consider our own contacts and make decisions about teaching and learning accordingly.

For too long, many of us have worked in many of the silos that exist in the educational landscape. We hope that this book will inspire curiosity for all of us to respectfully learn from one another. Our children cannot afford for us to continue in these silos and not engage in meaningful discourse, share effective research-based methods, and challenge one another while respecting our unique contexts. Ideally, we engage with one another while maintaining a curious stance, as practitioners who place a high value on science. As authors, we each came to this endeavor with two of us having had much experience in Montessori classrooms and another having had extensive experience in more conventional elementary classrooms. We packed up certainty and pride, as they had no place in our conversations, research, and work together. In his book *Think Again: The Power of Knowing What You Don't Know*, Adam Grant wrote,

> Scientific thinking favors humility over pride, doubt over certainty, curiosity over closure. When we shift out of scientist mode, the rethinking cycle breaks down, giving way to an overconfidence cycle. If we're preaching, we can't see gaps in our knowledge: we believe we've already found the truth. Pride breeds conviction rather than doubt, which makes us prosecutors: we might be laser-focused on changing other people's minds, but ours is set in stone. That launches us into confirmation bias and desirability bias. (p.28)

As you read this book, we hope that you were able to choose "humility over pride, doubt over certainty, and curiosity over closure" (Grant, 2021, p. 28). It is by taking this kind of stance that we can better advocate for *all* children to have access to powerful early literacy and reading instruction. We will not be serving our children well if we stay in our silos and choose pride over humility, certainty over doubt, and closure over curiosity. After all, as educators, we can meet our commitment to change the lives of children and impact the communities we serve in by following the science and by learning from one another.

References

Allsburg, C. V. (1995). *The sweetest fig*. Clarion Books.

Allsburg, C. V. (1984). *The mysteries of Harris Burdick*. Houghton Mifflin.

American Montessori Society. (2018). AMS School Accreditation Standards & Criteria. Standard 3: Teaching and Learning, Uninterrupted work periods for Early Childhood and Elementary programs (3.7.2 and 3.7.3, p. 7).

Anders, P. L., & Bos, C. S. (1986). Semantic feature analysis: An interactive strategy for vocabulary development text comprehension. *Journal of Reading, 29*, 610–617.

Archer, A. L., & Hughes, C. A. (2011). *Explicit instruction: Effective and efficient teaching*. Guilford Press.

Bahena, S. (2016). Differences as deficiencies—Persistence of the 30 million word gap. *IDRA Newsletter,* June–July, Intercultural Development Research Association.

Barrett, P., Zhang, Y., Moffatt, J., & Kobbacy, K. (2013). A holistic multi-level analysis identifying the impact of classroom design on pupils' learning. *Building and Environment, 59,* 678–689.

Beck, I. L., McKeown, M. G., & Kucan, L. (2015). *Creating robust vocabulary: Frequently asked questions and extended examples*. Guilford Press.

Becker, A. (2014). *Journey*. Candlewick Press.

Becker, A. (2015). *Quest*. Candlewick Press.

Becker, A. (2016). *Return*. Candlewick Press.

Beers, K. (2003). *When Kids Can't Read; What Teachers Can Do*. Heinemann.

Biemiller, A., & Slonim, N. (2001). Estimating root word vocabulary growth in normative and advantaged populations: Evidence for a common sequence of vocabulary acquisition. *Journal of Educational Psychology, 93,* 498–520. http://doi.org/10.1037/0022-0663.93.3.498.

Bourne, L. (2009). Grammar, what is it good for? *Montessori for Everyone Blog.* https://www.blog.montessoriforeveryone.com/grammar.html

Brady, S. (2020). A 2020 perspective on research findings on alphabetics (phoneme awareness and phonics): Implications for instruction (expanded version). *The Reading League Journal.* https://www.thereadingleague.org/wp-content/uploads/2020/10/Brady-Expanded-Version-of-Alphabetics-TRLJ.pdf

Brett, J. (1997). *The Hat*. Penguin Young Readers Group.

Brett, J. (2009). *The Mitten*. Penguin Young Readers Group.

Brett, J. (2018). *The Snowy Nap*. Penguin Young Readers Group.

Brown, K. J., Patrick, K. C., Fields, M. K., & Craig, G. T. (2021). Phonological awareness materials in Utah kindergartens: A case study in the Science of Reading. *Reading Research Quarterly, 56*(S1), p. S249-S272. International Literacy Association. http://doi.org/10.1002/rrq.386

Brunold-Conesa, C. (2021, November 12). Revisiting the Pink Tower: A pillar of pedagogical ingenuity. *Montessori Life*, American Montessori Society. https://amshq.org/Blog/2021_11_17-Revisiting-the-Pink-Tower-A-Pillar-of-Pedagogical-Ingenuity?successMessage=Thank%20you%20for%20joining%20our%20list

Cain, K. (2021, September 28). *The Reading Rope: A focus on verbal reasoning* [PowerPoint slides]. PaTTAN's 20th Celebration of Scarborough's Reading Rope. https://padlet-uploads.storage.googleapis.com/946193166/a951961f0e2f bb46a09bf3c7339e69b7/CAIN_ReadingRope_TO_SHOW.pdf

Canzoneri-Golden, L., & King, J. (2020). An examination of culturally relevant pedagogy and antibias-antiracist curriculum in a Montessori setting. Graduate-level student theses, dissertations, and portfolios, 360. https://spiral.lynn.edu/etds/360

Conway, C. M., Pisoni, D., & Kronenberger, W. G. (2009). The importance of sound for cognitive sequencing abilities: The auditory scaffolding hypothesis. *Current Directions in Psychological Science*, 18(5) 275–279.

Coyne, M. D., & Loftus-Rattan, S. M. (2022). Structured literacy interventions for vocabulary. In L. Spear-Swerling (Ed.), *Structured literacy interventions: Teaching students with reading difficulties, grades K-6* (pp. 114–135). Guilford Press.

Culclasure, B., Fleming, D., & Riga, G. (2018). *An evaluation of Montessori education in South Carolina's public schools*. The Riley Institute, Furman University.

Csikszentmihalyi, M. (1996). *Creativity*. HarperCollins.

Debs, M. (2019). *Diverse families, desirable schools: Public Montessori in the era of school choice*. Harvard University Press.

Delpit, L. (2006). *Other people's children: Cultural conflict in the classroom*. New Press.

Dwyer, M. (1970). *A key to reading and writing for English*. Nienhuis Montessori.

Dyslexia: A legislative information site. (2022, April). *State Dyslexia Laws*. https://www.dyslegia.com/state-dyslexia-laws/

Ehri, L. C. (2020). The science of learning to read words: A case for systematic phonics instruction. *Reading Research Quarterly*, 55(S1), S45–S60. http://doi.org/10.1002/rrq.334

Enz, B. J., & Morrow, L. M. (2009). *Assessing preschool literacy development: Informal and formal measures to guide instruction*. International Reading Association.

Fisher, D., & Frey, N. (2014). Speaking and listening in content area learning. *The Reading Teacher*, 68(1), 64–69. http://doi.org/10.1002/trtr.1296

Flaste, R. (October 8, 1989). The power of concentration. *The New York Times*, Section 6, p. 6. https://www.nytimes.com/1989/10/08/magazine/the-power-of-concentration.html

Foorman, B., Beyler, N., Borradaile, K., Coyne, M., Denton, C. A., Dimino, J., Furgeson, J., Hayes, L., Henke, J., Justice, L., Keating, B., Lewis, W., Sattar, S., Streke, A., Wagner, R., & Wissel, S. (2016). *Foundational skills to support reading for understanding in kindergarten through 3rd grade* (NCEE 2016-4008). National Center for Education Evaluation and Regional Assistance (NCEE), Institute of Education Sciences, U.S. Department of Education. http://whatworks.ed.gov

Frayer, D., Frederick, W. C., & Klausmeier, H. J. (1969). *A schema for testing the level of cognitive mastery*. Wisconsin Center for Education Research.

Gates, H. L. (2021, October 12). On literary freedom as an essential human right. *New York Times Book Review*. https://www.nytimes.com/2021/10/12/books/review/freedom-literary-expression-henry-louis-gates.html

Gilkerson, J., Richards, J. A., Warren, S. F., Montgomery, J. K., Greenwood, C. R., Kimbrough Oller, D., & Paul, T. D. (2017). Mapping the early language environment using all day recordings and automated analysis. *American Journal of Speech-Language Pathology, 26,* 248–265.

Golinkoff, R. M., Hoff, E., Rowe, M. L., Tamis-LeMonda, C. S., & Hirsh-Pasek, K. (2018). Language matters: Denying the existence of the 30-million-word gap has serious consequences. *Child Development, 90*(3), 985–992.

Goodman, A. (2005). The middle school high five: Strategies that can triumph. *Voices from the Middle, 13*(2), 12–19.

Goodman, K. S. (1970). Reading: A psycholinguistic guessing game. In H. Singer & R. B. Ruddell (Eds.), *Theoretical models and processes of reading* (pp. 497–508). International Reading Association.

Goswami, U. (2001). Early phonological development and the acquisition of literacy. In S. Neuman & D. Dickinson (Eds.), *Handbook of early literacy research, Vol 1* (pp. 97–110). Guilford Press.

Gough, P. B., & Tunmer, W. E. (1986). Decoding, reading and reading disability. *Remedial and Special Education, 7,* 6–10. https://doi:10.1177/074193258600700104

Grace, K. (2007). *Phonics and spelling through phoneme-grapheme mapping.* Sopris West Educational Services.

Grant, A. (2021). *Think again: The power of knowing what you don't know.* Viking, an imprint of Penguin Random House LLC.

Hart, B., & Risley, T. R. (1995). *Meaningful differences in the everyday experience of young American children.* Brookes Publishing.

Hattie, J. (2009). *Visible learning: A synthesis of over 800 meta-analyses relating to achievement.* Routledge.

Hirsch, E. D., & Wright, S. A. (2004). *Core knowledge.* Core Knowledge Foundation.

Hoover, W. A., & Tunmer, W. E. (2021). The primacy of science in communicating advances in the Science of Reading. *Reading Research Quarterly, 57*(2), 399–408. https://doi.org/10.1002/rrq.446

Hwang, H., Cabell, S. Q., & Joyner, R. E. (2021). Effects of integrated literacy and content-area instruction on vocabulary and comprehension in the elementary years: A meta-analysis. *Scientific Studies of Reading, 70*(1), 223–249., https://doi.org/10.1177/23813377211032195

James, K. H., & Atwood, T. P. (2009). The role of sensorimotor learning in the perception of letter-like forms: Tracking the causes of neural specialization for letters. *Cognitive Neuropsychology, 26*(1), 91–110.

Kamhi, A. G. (2007). Knowledge deficits: The true crisis in America. *The ASHA Leader,* (12)7, 28–29. The American Speech Language Hearing Association. https://leader.pubs.asha.org/doi/full/10.1044/leader.FMP.12072007.28

Keefe, J. W., & Jenkins, J. M. (2002). Two schools: Two approaches to personalized learning. *Phi Delta Kappan, 83*(6), 449–456.

Kilpatrick, D. (2021a, May 25). *Understanding sight-word recognition in Scarborough's Reading Rope* [PowerPoint slides]. PaTTAN's 20th Celebration of Scarborough's Reading Rope. https://www.youtube.com/watch?v=4O4V4bYKm_I

Kilpatrick, D. A. (2021b). *Equipped for reading success: A comprehensive, step-by-step program for developing phoneme awareness and fluent word recognition.* Casey & Kirsch Publishers.

Klemm, W. R. (2013, March 14). Why writing by hand could make you smarter. *Psychology Today*. https://www.psychologytoday.com/us/blog/memory-medic/201303/why-writing-hand-could-make-you-smarter

Knowledge Matters Campaign Scientific Advisory Committee. (2022). *Statement from the Knowledge Matters Campaign Scientific Advisory Committee*. StandardsWork, Inc. https://knowledgematterscampaign.org/statement-from-the-knowledge-matters-campaign-scientific-advisory-committee/?fbclid=IwAR2kIPRqpS88jYgEl_CHxtsI1tC0v7GcUGYokA3X6Qeq2L_2mYJwIYMQHB8

Ladson-Billings, G. (1995). Toward a theory of culturally relevant pedagogy. *American Educational Research Journal, 32*(3), 465–491. https://doi.org/10.3102/00028312032003465

Language and Reading Research Consortium & Logan, J. (2017). Pressure points in reading comprehension: A quantile multiple regression analysis. *Journal of Educational Psychology, 109*(4), 451–464. https://doi.org/10.1037/edu0000150

Lerner, M. D., & Lonigan, C. J. (2016). Bidirectional relations between phonological awareness and letter knowledge in preschool revisited: A growth curve analysis of the relation between two code-related skills. *Journal of Experimental Child Psychology, 144*, 166–183.

Lillard, A. S., Heise, M. J., Richey, E. M., Tong, X., Hart, A., & Bray, P. M. (2017). Montessori preschool elevates and equalizes child outcomes: A longitudinal study. *Frontiers in Psychology, 8*, 1783. https://www.frontiersin.org/articles/10.3389/fpsyg.2017.01783/full

Marcotte, K., McSween, M. P., Pouliot, M., Martineau, S., Pauzé, A. M., Wiseman-Hakes, C., & MacDonald, S. (2017). Normative study of the Functional Assessment of Verbal Reasoning and Executive Strategies (FAVRES) Test in the French-Canadian population. *Journal of Speech, Language, and Hearing Research, 60*, 2217–2227.

Marzano, R. J., Marzano, J. S., & Pickering, D. J. (2003). *Classroom management that works: Research-based strategies for every teacher*. Association for Supervision and Curriculum Development.

Maslen, B. L., & Maslen, J. R. (2006). *Bob Books, Set 1, Beginning Readers*. Scholastic.

Masonheimer, P. E., Drum, P. A., & Ehri, L. A. (1984). Does environmental print identification lead children into word reading? *Journal of Reading Behavior, 16*(4), 257–271.

Massaro, D. W. (2015). Two different communication genres and implications for vocabulary development and learning to read. *Journal of Literacy Research, 47*(4), 505–527. https://doi.org/10.1177/1086296X15627528

Mavrič, Maruša. (Fall 2020). The Montessori approach as a model of personalized instruction. *Journal of Montessori Research, 6*(2), 13–25.

McLoyd, V. C., & Purtell, K. M. (2008). How childhood poverty and income affect children's cognitive functioning and school achievement. In S. Neuman (Ed.), *Educating the other America: Top experts tackle poverty, literacy, and achievement in our schools* (pp. 52–73). Brookes.

Miller, A. C., & Keenan, J. M. (2009). How word decoding skill impacts text memory: The centrality deficit and how domain knowledge can compensate. *Annals of Dyslexia, 59*(2), 99–113. http://www.jstor.org/stable/23765203

Moats, L. C. (1998). Teaching decoding. *American Educator, 22*(1), 42–49.

Moats, L. C. (2020). *Speech to print language essentials for teachers.* Paul H. Brookes Publishing.

Moats, L. (2022). Structured language interventions for spelling. In L. Spear-Swerling (Ed.), *Structured literacy interventions: Teaching students with reading difficulties, grades K–6, 67–94.* Guilford Press.

Moats, L. C., & Tolman, C. A. (2019). *LETRS Volume 2* (3rd ed.). Voyager Sopris Learning, Inc.

Moll, L. C., Amanti, C., Neff, D., & Gonzalez, N. (1992). Funds of knowledge for teaching: Using a qualitative approach to connect homes and classrooms. *Theory into Practice, 31*(2), 132–141. https://doi.org/10.1080/00405849209543534

Montessori, M. (1916/1965). *Spontaneous activity in education. Vol. 1 of the Advanced Montessori Method.* Schocken.

Montessori, M. (1947/2019). *Citizen of the world: Key Montessori readings.* Pierson Publishing.

Montessori, M. (1948/1967). *The discovery of the child.* [Trans. M. J. Costelloe]. Ballantine Books.

Montessori, M. (1949/1967). *The absorbent mind.* Holt, Rinehart & Winston.

Montessori, M. (1965). *Dr. Montessori's own handbook.* Schocken Books.

Montessori, M. (1985). *To educate the human potential,* 6th edition. Kalakshetra Publications.

Montessori, M. (2012). *The 1946 London lectures.* Montessori-Pierson Publishing Co.

Montessori, M., & Joosten, A. M. (2004). *The formation of man.* Clio.

Murdoch, A., Warburg, R., Corbo, E., & Strickler, W. (2021). Project Ready! An early literacy program to close the readiness gap for children living in poverty. *Reading & Writing Quarterly,* (38)4, 340–358. http://doi.org/10.1080/10573569.2021.1954570

Murphy, M. (2016). Foreword. In M. Murphy, S. Redding, & J. S. Twyman (Eds.), *Handbook on personalized learning for states, districts, and schools* (pp. i–vi). Center on Innovations for Learning, Information Age Publishing.

National Center for Montessori in the Public Sector. (2021). *Montessori census.* https://www.montessoricensus.org/

National Early Literacy Panel. (2008). *Developing early literacy: Report of the National Early Literacy Panel.* National Institute for Literacy.

National Governors Association Center for Best Practices & Council of Chief State School Officers. (2010). *Common Core State Standards for English language arts and literacy in history/social studies, science, and technical subjects.* Authors.

National Institute of Child Health and Human Development. (2000). *Report of the National Reading Panel. Teaching children to read: An evidence-based assessment of the scientific research literature on reading and its implications for reading instruction* (NIH Publication No. 00-4769). U.S. Government Printing Office.

National Research Council (NRC) and the Committee on the Prevention of Reading Difficulties in Young Children, Snow, C. E., Burns, S. M., & Griffin, P. (1998). *Preventing reading difficulties in young children.* National Academy Press.

National Scientific Council on the Developing Child. (2004). *Young children develop in an environment of relationships* (Working Paper No. 1). http://developingchild.harvard.edu/index.php/library/reports_and_working_papers/working_papers/wp1/

Neuman, S. B. (2021). *Vocabulary development*. Patten Literacy Expert Series, July 27, 2021. https://www.youtube.com/watch?v=3FKEBsWgeAM

Neuman, S. B., & Roskos, K. (1997). Literacy knowledge in practice: Contexts of participation for young writers and readers. *Reading Research Quarterly, 32*, 10–32. https://doi.org/10.1598/RRQ.32.1.2

Olsen, J. Z., Fink, C., & Marxer, M. (2003). *Handwriting without tears*. Cabin John, MD, Publisher.

Paris, D., & Alim, H. S. (Eds.). (2017). *Culturally sustaining pedagogies: Teaching and learning for justice in a changing world*. Teachers College Press.

Pondiscio, R. (2021, April 16). *Can teaching be improved by law?* Education Next. https://www.educationnext.org/can-teaching-be-improved-by-law-twenty-states-measures-reading/

Ose Askvik, E., van der Weel, F. R., & van der Meer, A. L. H. (2020). The importance of cursive handwriting over typewriting for learning in the classroom: A high-density EEG study of 12-year-old children and young adults. *Frontiers in Psychology, 11*, 1–16. https://www.frontiersin.org/articles/10.3389/fpsyg.2020.01810/full

Rathunde, K. (2015). Creating a context for flow: The importance of personal insight and experience. *The NAMTA Journal, (40)*3, 15–27. https://files.eric.ed.gov/fulltext/EJ1077078.pdf

Reading League. (2021). *The science of reading: A defining guide*. Defining Guide eBook. https://www.thereadingleague.org/what-is-the-science-of-reading/defining-guide-ebook/

Recht, D. R., & Leslie, L. (1988). Effect of prior knowledge on good and poor readers' memory of text. *Journal of Educational Psychology, 80*(1), 16–20.

Reutzel, D. R., Fawson P., Young, J., Morrison, R., Timothy, G., & Wilcox, B. (2003). Reading environmental print: What is the role of concepts about print in discriminating young readers' responses? *Reading Psychology* (pp. 123–162).

Rhode Island Board of Education. (1917). *Forty-seventh annual report of the state board of education together with the seventy-second annual report of the commissioner of public schools of Rhode Island*. Hamilton Press. https://hdl.handle.net/2027/coo.31924101114795

Romeo, R. R., Leonard, J. A., Robinson, S. T., West, M. R., Mackey, A. P., Rowe, M. L., & Gabrieli, J. D. (2018). Beyond the 30-million-word gap: Children's conversational exposure is associated with language-related brain function. *Psychological Science, 29*(5), 700–710.

Rosenblatt, L. M. (1978). *The reader, the text, the poem: The transactional theory of the literary work*. Southern Illinois University Press.

Rosenshine, B. (1987). Explicit teaching and teacher training. *Journal of Teacher Education, 38*(3), 34–36. https://doi.org/10.1177/002248718703800308

Scarborough, H. S. (2001). Connecting early language and literacy to later reading (dis)abilities: Evidence, theory, and practice. In S. Neuman & D. Dickinson (Eds.), *Handbook for research in early literacy* (pp. 97–110). Guilford Press.

Schneider, W., Körkel, J., & Weinert, F. (1989). Domain-specific knowledge and memory performance: A comparison of high- and low-aptitude children. *Journal of Educational Psychology, 81*, 306–312. http://doi.org/10.1037/0022-0663.81.3.306

Sedita, Joan (2022). Orthographic mapping. *Resource Directory, Houston Branch of the International Dyslexia Association*. https://284ivp1abr6435y6t219n54e

-wpengine.netdna-ssl.com/wp-content/uploads/2022/03/Orthographic-Mapping -HBIDA-Article.pdf

Segers, E., & Verhoeven, L. (2016). How logical reasoning mediates the relation between lexical quality and reading comprehension. *Reading and Writing*, 29(4), 577–590. https://doi.org/doi10.1007/s11145-015-9613-9

Séguin, É. (1866). *Idiocy and its treatment by the physiological method*. William Wood & Co. https://wellcomecollection.org/works/rnxtfst6/items?canvas=7

Seidenberg, M. S., & McClelland, J. L. (1989). A distributed, developmental model of word recognition and naming. *Psychological Review*, 96(4), 523–568. https://doi .org/10.1037/0033-295x.96.4.523

Shanahan, T. (2022). *Grammar and comprehension: Scaffolding student interpretation of complex sentences*. Shanahan on Literacy. https://www.shanahanonliteracy .com/blog/grammar-and-comprehension-scaffolding-student-interpretation-of -complex-sentences#sthash.uHW7znJv.dpbs

Smith, R., Snow, P., Serry, T., & Hammond, L. (2021). The role of background knowledge in reading comprehension: A critical review. *Reading Psychology*, 42(3), 214–240, http://doi.org/10.1080/02702711.2021.1888348

Spear-Swerling, L. (2019). Structured literacy and typical literacy practices: Understanding differences to create instructional opportunities. *Teaching Exceptional Children*, 51(3), 201–211.

Standing, E. M. (1957/1998). *Maria Montessori: Her life and work*. Penguin Putnam Inc.

Stanford Children's Health. (n.d.) *Age-appropriate speech and hearing milestones*. https://www.stanfordchildrens.org/en/topic/default?id=age-appropriate-speech -and-hearing-milestones-90-P02169

Stanovich, K. E. (1986). Matthew effects in reading: Some consequences of individual differences in the acquisition of literacy. *Reading Research Quarterly*, 22, 360–407.

Stanovich, K. E. (1993). Does reading make you smarter? Literacy and the development of verbal intelligence. In H. Reese (Ed.), *Advances in child development and behavior*, 24, 133–180. Academic Press.

Stone, L. (2020). *Orthographic mapping explainer* [Video]. YouTube. https://youtube /KIuwKnZqJEQ

Suskind, D. (2015). *Thirty million words: Building a child's brain*. Dutton/Penguin Books.

Texas Center for Reading and Language Arts. (2002). *Effective Instruction Walkthrough: Explicit Systematic Instruction*. Second grade teacher academy. https:// ceedar.education.ufl.edu/wp-content/uploads/2016/03/Reading-Handout-2.2.pdf

Thornbury, S. (1999). *How to teach grammar*. Longman.

Tzuriel, D., Isman, E. B., Klung, T., & Haywood, H.C. (2017). Effects of teaching classification, verbal conceptualization, and analogic reasoning in children with developmental delays. *Journal of Cognitive Education and Psychology*, 16(1), 107–124.

United Nations General Assembly. (1989). *Convention on the Rights of the Child*, Treaty Series, vol. 1577, p. 3.

U.S. Department of Education, Institute of Education Sciences, National Center for Education Statistics, National Assessment of Educational Progress (NAEP). (2019). *NAEP Report Card: 2019 NAEP Reading Assessment*. https://www.nationsreport card.gov/highlights/reading/2019/

Vacca, R. T., Vacca, J. A. L., & Mraz, M. (2021). *Content area reading: Literacy and learning across the curriculum.* Pearson.

VanHekken, A., Bottari, M., & Heggerty, M. (2020). *Bridge the gap: Phonemic awareness intervention lessons.* Literacy Resources, LLC.

Vaughn, S., Gersten, R., Dimino, J., Taylor, M. J., Newman-Gonchar, R., Krowka, S., Kieffer, M. J., McKeown, M., Reed, D., Sanchez, M., St. Martin, K., Wexler, J., Morgan, S., Yañez, A., & Jayanthi, M. (2022). *Providing reading interventions for students in grades 4–9* (WWC 2022007). National Center for Education Evaluation and Regional Assistance (NCEE), Institute of Education Sciences, U.S. Department of Education. https://whatworks.ed.gov/

Vukelich, C., & Christie, J. (2009). *Building a foundation for preschool literacy: Effective instruction for children's reading and writing development* (2nd ed.) International Reading Association.

Walberg, H. J., & Tsai, S.-l. (1983). Matthew effects in education. *American Educational Research Journal, 20*(3), 359–373. https://doi.org/10.2307/1162605

Walker, D., Greenwood, C., Hart, B., & Carta, J. (1994). Prediction of school outcomes based on early language production and socioeconomic factors. *Child Development, 65,* 606–621

Walton Family Foundation (2018). *Walton Family Foundation Announces investments to fuel high-quality school growth nationwide.* https://www.waltonfamilyfoundation.org/about-us/newsroom/major-investments-to-fuel-high-quality-school-growth-nationwide

Washington, J. A., & Seidenberg. M.S. (2021). *Teaching reading to African American children.* https://www.aft.org/ae/summer2021/washington_seidenberg

Wilborn, S. (2020). *Reading SOS: How can I get my four-year-old to learn more words?* Reading Rockets [Video]. YouTube. https://www.youtube.com/watch?v=B_vWuPVquLw&t=93s

Willingham, D. (2006). *How knowledge helps.* https://www.aft.org/periodical/american-educator/spring-2006/how-knowledge-helps

Willingham, D. T. (2009). *Why don't students like school? A cognitive scientist answers questions about how the mind works and what it means for the classroom.* Jossey-Bass.

Wilson, B. A. (2012). *Fundations: Wilson language basics* (2nd ed.). Wilson Language Training Corporation.

Wolf, M., & Stoodley, C. J. (2017). *Proust and the squid: The story and science of the reading brain.* Harper Collins.

Zoll, S. The Montessori experiment in Rhode Island (1913–1940): Tracing theory to implementation over 25 years. (2017). *Journal of Montessori Research, 3*(2), 49–54. https://files.eric.ed.gov/fulltext/EJ1161330.pdf

Index

About the Authors

Dr. Susan Zoll is associate professor and co-coordinator of the Early Childhood Education (Birth-2nd grade) program at Rhode Island College. She has served in leadership roles on several Early Reading First projects (ERF, 2004, 2006, 2009) funded by the U.S. Department of Education, and her work on the development of Personal Literacy Plans, a tool to share individualized assessment outcomes with teachers and families, was recognized by the *Doing What Works* initiative. Her dissertation, "From 'At Risk' to 'At Promise': An Evaluation of an Early Reading First Project," speaks to the need for increased access to high-quality early language and literacy opportunities to prepare all children for reading success.

Dr. Zoll holds a 3–6 Montessori credential (AMS) and has served as a classroom teacher, a teacher trainer for the Language curriculum, and a Head of School. Her recent research includes historical analysis of early adopters of Montessori education (2017), the development of a Montessori logic model to inform education research (2019), and an overview of assessment and observation practices in Montessori classrooms (2023).

Dr. Natasha Feinberg is an assistant professor at Rhode Island College in the Elementary Education Department. She instructs preservice teachers in the areas of reading and writing and also directs the Master's of Education in Reading program. With an Ed.D. in curriculum leadership from Northeastern University, Dr. Feinberg has 17 years of experience as a reading specialist/literacy coach in the Rhode Island public school system. Her area of expertise lies in the Science of Reading and teaching reading to all types of learners. She has worked extensively with Tier 2 and Tier 3 literacy interventions identifying specific student literacy needs and matching evidence-based interventions and specific progress-monitoring tools that address those needs. Her work focuses on supporting data-based individualization and data-based decision-making.

Dr. Laura Saylor is dean of the School of Education at Mount St. Joseph University. She earned her Ph.D. in educational studies with a concentration in educational policy and higher education with a focus in STEM education from the University of Cincinnati. Previously, she earned her Master's of Education from Xavier University with a concentration in Montessori education.

Her 25 years of practical experience include teaching in inclusive and multi-age settings and serving as the Head of School for an independent Montessori school. Dr. Saylor is a frequent presenter at national conferences. Her research foci include the importance of learning and reading science in teacher preparation as well as assessing performance of preservice teachers in clinical experiences. Dr. Saylor's interests also extend to best practices in educational assessment, and collaborative work between P–12 and educator preparation. Her recently published research includes mathematics discourse with preservice teachers and the effects of teacher-centered mentorship.